THE COST OF LIGHT

The Cost of Light

Clauthia Rai Fields

The Cost of LightA Memoir of Shadows and Fire

B^{y:}

Clauthia Rai Fields

Copyright Page

Published by Ink & Reign Publishing, an imprint of RaiStone Publishing

ISBN (Paperback): 979-8-9933335-0-2
ISBN (eBook): 979-8-9933335-1-9

Cover design by: Clauthia Rai. Fields

The events and conversations in this memoir are drawn from the author's own experiences and recollections. Some names and identifying details have been changed to protect privacy.
For more information

www.RaiStoneFoundation.org   www.RaiStoneRetreats.org

RaiStone Wellness Foundation

RaiStone Retreats

Dedication

F or my mother and my sister.

For my mother, my star and my sister, my heart.

RaiStone Wellness Foundation, born from your legacy.

Acknowledgment

To all my family—thank you for walking this life with me and for standing strong.

To my mother, the Star, thank you for your energy. I never knew I would love and cherish it so much. You were a star in a world that couldn't see you.

To my sister—I wish I could have been more for you. I love you. I see you. And I miss you.

To my nephew—the one who taught me to love. Pain has kept us apart, but you are the reason I live. You were the courage I didn't know I had. I thought I was protecting you, but it was you who showed me what love is.

To my childhood friends—I believe God walked us together for a reason. I will always love, value, and see you for the light you were and still are in my life.

To the teachers and coaches who saw me—thank you. Your light gave me the drive to shine a light of my own, exponentially.

To my children—I know we are not perfect, but I pray you feel seen, loved, guided, and held in every choice you make. Rely on God. He will never leave you. Even in the dark, He is there.

And to my husband—the biggest flashlight I know. You have always wanted me in the light. It's been so hard to step into it, but only God knows how deeply I appreciate the light you've always been. I love you.

Author's Note

I wrote this book as a young Black woman who refused to stay in the dark. Every page was a return, a reckoning, a release. The shadows I lived through were real—but so is the light. This is my offering to anyone who has ever whispered in silence.

Prologue

The Cost of Light

For so many years I have dreamed and focused on doing what's right—the right choice, the safe choice, the next choice. 100 miles and running is what my label could be for many that know me. I have gotten more done in my lifetime than many, and sometimes even more than one.

But what I didn't have was pause and reflection. I never stopped to even wonder: am I safe? Is this right? Is this exactly what I want? No—most of my life has been spent running towards what I called the light.

But what I have learned in my just-shy-of-50 years is that running to the light has a cost, a price that you pay. So this memoir is about my run—about my cost.

I ran so much I hid parts of me. I have been a liar, a thief—not fake, as I was always real—but fake to myself, because I didn't let myself be all of who I was. I have hidden parts of me that made me feel ashamed or wrong. But stepping into the light requires a true embracement of all you are. And only through that darkness can you actually move into the light.

So, in a sense, this whole time I have been running to the light while shielding and protecting the very darkness that held me, the very darkness that scared me. It's almost as if I was running and holding my own umbrella of darkness. But I understand more now, and why I needed not to hide, not to shield, and why I need to let that umbrella go to truly be safe, to truly feel the light.

This is my story—of how it took me almost 50 years to realize how to find that light. So I hope this helps someone, helps you understand your goods and your bads, and helps you become whole.

Table of Contents

Table of Contents
Chapter One: The Kitchen Confrontation
Chapter Two: A New Beginning in California
Chapter Three: The Absent Father
Chapter Four: Sister's Silent Struggles
Chapter Five: The Visit of the Vampire
Chapter Six: The Green Hill, The Gun, and The Cousins
Chapter Seven: The Hidden Gymnast
Chapter Eight: Paper and a Flashlight
Chapter Nine: The Girl Who Sang Better Than Whitney
Chapter Ten: The House
Chapter Eleven: The Purple Room and the Hidden Vampire
Chapter Twelve: Middle School Beginnings
Chapter Thirteen: The Last Time We Were Little Girls
Chapter Fourteen: Eighth Grade Milestones
Chapter Fifteen: The Cost of Light
Chapter Sixteen: The Riot and the Stage
Chapter Seventeen: The Discovery of Loss
Chapter Eighteen: Strength and Shadow
Chapter Nineteen: The Cop, the Hammer, and the Exit Wound
Chapter Twenty: The Mirror

One

The Kitchen Confrontation

The industrial, low hum of the fridge was the most reliable sound in my grandmother's entire Memphis house. It was a mechanical, holding-pattern noise that provided a deceptive blanket of normalcy—a low thrumming designed to mask the constant, high-pitched tension of the human lives being lived within its walls. I was four years old, a small, demanding creature focused on a single, crystalline desire: a grape. The linoleum floor, cool and smooth beneath my bare feet, offered a welcome, grounding shock in the soft, humid atmosphere of the Sunday afternoon. My tiny stomach was already responding to the rich, deep, slow-cooked scent of Grandma's spaghetti—a complex, layered siren call of garlic, herbs, and simmering tomato that promised comfort and fullness. Yet, all that mattered in that moment was reaching the cold metal handle, stretching every fiber of my small body upward, fingers desperately seeking purchase. One grape. Just one.

Before that precise moment, my life was a physical manifestation of freedom. The outside world—the backyards, the cracked pavement, the dusty alleys—was my genuine sanctuary, a boundless space where my body felt invincible. I didn't recognize fear in the act of movement. Leaping was natural, landing was secondary, and falling was merely a brief interruption. I was relentless: I skated until my calves burned, I ran until my breath hitched, and I climbed trees that scraped my skin until they bled. I always, always got back up. This external world felt vast, open, and wholly receptive to my fierce energy—it was the pure, unadulterated sensation of freedom, and that freedom vibrated like a plucked wire deep within the marrow of my bones.

The indoors, by contrast, felt like a cage woven of unspoken rules. It was perpetually tight, constrained, and demanded a stifling conformity. It was quiet, yes, but held none of the weightless quality of peace. It was stiff, controlled, constantly forcing me to negotiate my own size, making me shrink. The outside let me soar; the inside required me to hide my wings.

My companion, Boy Rai, and I communicated with the telepathy of true partnership. Our language was built entirely on action and shared understanding: "Wanna ride?" "Yeah, let's ride." "Wanna jump?" "Yeah, let's jump." We lived in perpetual motion, our communication conveyed through the effortless language of nodded agreement and shared, uninhibited laughter. We weren't truly named Rai, but that nickname captured our shared exuberance. I, with my middle name Rainette (a nod to my mother's beloved Corvette Stingray), and my sister, Lavette, were, literally, the products of fast dreams and faster, life-altering decisions.

My appearance was itself a form of subtle defiance. My hair, always carefully braided, hung free in the breeze like small, celebratory flags behind me. My clothing was soft, light, and, most importantly, cut for relentless movement. Mama, with her meticulous skill, made them herself. Though I couldn't articulate the word couture, I felt implicitly and powerfully tailored. The clothes were intentionally roomy, designed to breathe, stitched with care and an intention that made them feel peaceful, small perhaps, but somehow big enough to contain all of me.

But in that kitchen, on the cusp of reaching that grape, all of that hard-won freedom was instantly, brutally frozen.

A thick, intrusive shadow fell across my small form—Uncle Curtis. The air around him was heavy, carrying a suffocating combination of

Old Spice, sour cigarette smoke, and the faint, chemical bitterness of mothballs. He didn't gently nudge me; he shoved me aside with deliberate force, his arm a solid, unyielding wall against my desperate reach.

"Get out of the way, girl," he growled, the single word girl weighted with a profound, casual dismissal that resonated deeper than a simple rebuke.

My lip began to tremble, but the response that rose within me was not fear. It was a hot, sudden, volcanic heat—an unfamiliar, righteous anger that bubbled up from my core. It flew out of my mouth before my conscious mind could measure the danger or contain the sound:

"Who the fuck do you think you are?"

The entire room dissolved into a silence so immediate and dense it seemed to crackle. It was the aftermath of a sonic boom, heavy and thick, punctuated only by the lingering echo of my curse. My mother and father, frozen in the doorway, their laughter violently cut off, stared at the scene—their expressions a complex, terrifying mixture of shock and dawning recognition.

I stood there, small and trembling, utterly bewildered. I didn't know the dictionary meaning of the curse word, but I understood its function: it was a weapon of absolute power. It had ripped the tension wide open, forcing an acknowledgment of the transgression.

At four years old, questions of identity were abstract. But I knew this: I had acted. I had spoken. Loudly. Sharply. Unfiltered.

And the world, paralyzed by the audacity of my voice, was unable to stop me.

They laughed. Not with cruelty, but with an astonishing mix of surprise, recognition, and a reluctant awe. In that complex, loaded sound, I received two simultaneous, terrifying lessons: the world might sometimes find my pain funny, but my unbridled voice—raw and shocking as it was—could either save me or cost me everything. The choice, and the danger, was mine.

My mother's eyes, even as her mouth smiled, held the deepest lesson. There was an ancient, weighty knowing behind them, a silent communication I couldn't comprehend at four. But now, I know that was the undeniable moment the baton was passed. It was the silent, profound burden of becoming the one who would always fight back, the one who would roar. She knew, in that instant, that she wouldn't have to worry about her baby girl facing this world undefended.

My father, slim and richly brown like the cocoa-dark wood of our kitchen chairs, stood tall beside my mother. He and Uncle Curtis were physically similar, yet their presence represented two different worlds. Daddy was warm and grounding; Uncle Curtis possessed a pale quality—a lack of color that felt less like softness and more like a stark, immediate warning. The context of their differing shades, the complicated history they represented, would fundamentally shape my perceptions and the choices of those around me for decades.

I cannot recall what I finally ate that day. Perhaps I never even got that grape. But I remember, with perfect sensory clarity, the sheer force of my feeling—small, yes, but irrevocably not silent. Afraid, but powerfully not invisible.

That is the true beginning of my story. It starts not with a gentle fade, but with a question. A curse. And the defiant sound of a small girl who had just claimed the ferocious, unpredictable freedom of the wind.

Interlude: The Illusion of Order

My mother's perfectionism was not the casual, aesthetic obsession displayed in magazine pages or on social media. Hers was a relentless, militaristic pursuit of control. It manifested in every fiber of our home: every kitchen drawer was labeled, every wire hanger matched its mate, and every single room was maintained with the precise, untouchable austerity of a magazine spread. Our house did not look lived in. It looked staged. And that was not an accident. It was the point.

She kept everything spotless, perpetually ordered, perpetually prepared, because it was the singular area of her life—and her life's painful history—that she could command. She fought chaos with chlorine and fear with flawless folding.

As a child, I didn't understand the psychological urgency behind her actions. I only knew that I existed in a state of perpetually failing to measure up to her standard. She was a five-foot-tall, tiny, flawless force of nature—an Olivia Pope with sharp heels and suits pressed to impossible creases. Her body itself was part of the uniform; she wore a size zero my entire life, and even that was often large on her diminutive frame. She had learned to sew at a young age, a skill that wasn't a hobby but a fundamental requirement for achieving her standard of perfection. She had to customize everything. When I was small, I genuinely believed her tiny frame was inherently tailor-made. I noticed the difference in how she presented versus how others did, yet I never processed this through the lens of body image issues. As an adult, I understand that her daily look was a meticulously constructed shield. If the world wouldn't offer her safety and order, she would engineer it herself.

And she was terrifyingly successful. She rebuilt every single house we ever lived in from the studs up, drafting blueprints by hand, tearing down walls, and tackling Home Depot like it was a high-end couture boutique. She lived by a dogma that nothing in the physical world was unfixable. Nothing was too far gone to be salvaged, sanded, and repainted.

Except, perhaps, the emotional reality of our lives.

As a child, I believed she was imbued with magic. As an adult, I recognize the deep, enduring pain beneath the surface: her perfectionism was a coping strategy woven into the very fabric of her survival.

I inherited this curse. I have spent the better part of my adulthood waging an active war against the impossible standard she unwittingly passed down to me. The compulsion to perfect everything became my primary defense mechanism, my personal shield insulating me from the chaos I saw shatter everyone else. It was my version of the "right choice, the safe choice."

My mother was brilliant—a self-taught accountant, a savvy business starter, an unstoppable fixer. But her entire philosophy was contained within the now, the immediate, controllable surface. She had no discernible philosophy for the future. When she died, she left me a modest $10,000, yet her estate was buried under a mountain of bills. This woman, who likely spent millions in her lifetime through sheer will and drive, had left absolutely no provision for the future.

She cared only that everything looked right. And that, the realization that the perfection was a hollow defense, is what finally broke my need to emulate her.

My husband, Willie, is the steady counterpoint to my inherited chaos. He is the one who constantly reminds me, "Let it go. It's not covered." And I still find myself screaming back, silently, deep in my gut: It has to be covered. Because that is what I was implicitly taught. It wasn't taught in words, but in the frantic polishing of floors at midnight. It was taught in the elaborate birthday parties we couldn't afford and in the houses built from nothing, held together purely by throw pillows and my mother's terrifying willpower.

This memoir is where I begin the deliberate, difficult act of breaking that generational cycle.

I will no longer chase her impossible perfection.
 I seek provision.
I seek peace.

The only way forward is to stop running the race she began and finally admit that some things—especially the most vital things—cannot be fixed by force, but must be accepted in love.

Two

A New Beginning in California

The final weeks in Memphis were characterized by a pressure so intense it felt physical. Everything was too tight, too small, too volatile. It was palpable in the air, dense and suffocatingly humid, and visible in the painful rigidity of my mother's jaw. I was only four, yet I possessed an uncanny, almost animalistic sensitivity to the emotional barometer of the house. I knew, without having the words for it, that the feeling residing in my stomach was a deep, paralyzing knot of wrongness.

The trauma had preceded the physical escape. My earliest memories were composed of fragmented, violent snapshots: the sudden, deep-chested boom of my father's voice, the silence of Mama's music being replaced by the sound of smashing dishware, and the final, terrible quiet that followed her sobs—a silence that felt heavy enough to crush a small girl. These chaotic memories defined the world before my fourth birthday, the world we were finally, decisively leaving behind.

The small, defiant victory I'd won in the kitchen with my curse was nothing more than a spark. It wasn't enough to hold back the tension that was now a constant, mounting presence. Mama had reached a place of ultimate clarity: she'd had enough. Her husband's escalating violence, the paralyzing unpredictability of his mood storms—it was a life she refused to continue. She wanted something more than that fragile existence. She chose, with the fierce certainty that defined her, to leave.

One day, the escape was real. We were suddenly, irreversibly, in the car. Mama was behind the wheel, driving us relentlessly west, pointing the car toward a new horizon and the promise of a clean, unwritten slate. Lisa and I were crammed into the backseat, the windows cranked down, the hot wind whipping my hair into a frenzy. I didn't know our exact destination, but I remember looking up at the sky and feeling that it was vast, endless, bigger than anything I'd ever known. It carried an unspoken, intoxicating hope: that maybe something good, something truly safe, could finally happen there.

California was Mama's chosen word for our freedom: a "new beginning." Los Angeles arrived in my vision as a glittering, strange toy city, a land of impossible, shimmering promise. The sun felt different, heavier with optimism, and the air carried the scent of salt mixed with something sweet—the smell of oranges, a scent I would only learn to name later.

In this new, terrifying world, Mama began to unfurl. She smiled more easily. She played music again, loud and vibrant, and sang along with uninhibited joy. We shared the safe, warm space of her bed just to talk and laugh. In those moments, she felt impossibly huge—a giant, even though she was barely five feet tall. She was our entire world, contained within one tiny, intensely fierce woman.

Her packing was deliberate. She packed culture, color, and sheer possibility. Photos and music were our essential lifeline. She was a creator—a painter, a singer, a maker—and she taught me, through her every action, that imagination was the deepest form of survival, that art was the only reliable path through darkness. Even when we were financially poor—a reality that only became clear to me much later—she made our life feel rich simply by the sheer force of her creative will.

She painted over the pain with color and imagination.

After the initial trauma of the break, life started to move in dizzying, unpredictable segments. We landed in East LA, when I was four, and our first accommodation was a single room rented from a massive, sprawling Hispanic family. This phase was defined by the sensory overload of instability: the dark, sudden gleam of roaches, the constant noise of children spilling out of every doorway, and the mix of Spanish and cartoons that became the backdrop of my days.

The little freedom I had was always found in my ritual: I'd eat a few bites of cereal on the cool linoleum, then be yanked by an irresistible need to be outside, barefoot on the hot concrete, chasing an untainted sense of movement. I was always chasing freedom.

This fragile freedom shattered when we moved into our own place, the Green Hill house, during my kindergarten year. It sat high on the incline, watching everything below. The move to this complex new beginning coincided with the onset of profound, terrifying instability. It was here that my sister, Lisa, went to stay with our aunt in San Francisco. When she returned, she was no longer a child. She was loud, angry, and impossibly grown—the immediate, visible result of the trauma she endured there.

The chaos soon became physical. The Red Brick Daycare was located near our Green Hill house, a place that taught me a different kind of terror. The workers, with chilling conviction, threatened us: if we didn't sleep, they would put tarantulas on us. I believed them utterly. I learned to clamp my eyes shut, lying perfectly still, paralyzed by fear. It was here I learned the dark wisdom of that trauma: not to move, not to react, to become invisible.

The random violence soon followed. One day, playing, Lisa found a gun. Mama was sitting in the rocking chair, on the phone. The bang was sharp, instantaneous. Mama didn't scream. She didn't shout. She just looked down at the sudden bloom of red on her leg and stated flatly, "I think I've been shot." Her silence and her numbness were more terrifying than any scream could have been; it filled the huge gap where a normal reaction to pain should have been heard.

We moved across the street soon after, but the arguing continued, the tension thicker than ever. I spent hours outside, riding my bike, desperate to chase down some lost peace. It was here, during a fight with a girl who followed Lisa home, that Mama—all 4'11" and 90 pounds of her—stood like an immovable fortress in the doorway. She became the wall.

This was my turbulent childhood in East LA: fragments of wild joy overlaid with the rising storm of silence and new, constant trauma. I was always somewhere in between the beautiful fantasy and the painful reality, forever trying to catch a clean breath.

Three

The Absent Father

The man I called Daddy was never a steady feature of my child-hood landscape. I couldn't construct an image of him built on the constancy of a routine or the reliable comfort of a permanent presence. All I held were isolated sensory fragments: the precise blend of his scent—aftershave, cigarettes, and the faint, nostalgic odor of diesel fuel. I knew his car—always dusty, always with the music playing low enough to suggest a private, guarded world. I knew the specific, tender sound of his voice when he said, "baby girl." But that was the entirety of my inventory.

When I tried to conjure him, my mind offered a hazy silhouette, like looking through glass streaked and blurred by rain. He was present in my narrative only as a periodic event, not a continuous existence. He would appear suddenly, like unexpected weather, and then vanish. He was never steady. Never home. Never a concept I could genuinely anchor my young heart to. I learned early that crying when he left was pointless; the more effective survival strategy was to simply stop expecting his return. This fortress, built on the painful foundation of low expectations, was my very first lesson in self-preservation.

Yet, my older sister, Lisa, carried a fuller, richer narrative. She had eight full years with him, a period of constancy and affection that defined her memory of him. She remembered the "soft parts," his consistent kindness, and the security of his protection. He called her "baby girl" with a steady, unwavering rhythm I never witnessed. She told me later that he would sing her to sleep, his low, comforting voice a profound contrast to the booming thunder I remembered from the last days in Memphis. For a period of her life, she had a steady father. And she needed that desperately.

For me, the connection remained a series of fleeting snapshots.

I remember the hug when I was five. We had traveled back to Memphis for a visit, and I wore a bright yellow sweater Mama had sent from LA, a subtle piece of evidence meant to remind him of our new reality. My heart hammered with nervous excitement as his car appeared. He hugged me. "Hey, baby girl," he said, and that embrace was everything: a confirmation, a moment of fleeting warmth. But when I asked to stay the night, the answer was the familiar caveat: "Not tonight, baby." I tried to hide my disappointment, forcing a brave smile, but my chest folded inward. I couldn't interpret the hesitation, so I internalized the meaning: I was either too much to handle or still not quite enough to hold.

At six, we returned again, and this time, the answer shifted: he allowed me to stay. He had constructed a new life. I met Anne, his partner, who wore clothes that shimmered and smelled like simple hairspray and sweet things. My older stepbrothers initiated me into the mysteries of video game football. I fumbled, felt silly, but they were kind, guiding me through the mechanics of the game. We laughed. We played. It was a new, fragile flicker of inclusion. I remember him protecting me when one of the boys changed the cartoon I was watching. "Let her watch what she wants," he said, and in that single, small act, I registered the most profound version of love: a moment of true, paternal presence.

The final time I saw him, I was seven years old, firmly established in the second grade. We had recently moved again, now to Inglewood, specifically to be closer to Mama's job at Centinela Hospital. He was there, in the hospital, and we went to see him. The room was cold, the lights harshly fluorescent, and the air was sterile, heavy with the metallic tang of bleach. He looked thin, reduced by illness, appearing as if the huge bed were slowly swallowing him whole. His voice was faint, barely a whisper, but he managed the phrase: "Hey, baby girl." He reached for my hand, and I held it. Mama stood by the door, her entire posture radiating stiffness. We didn't linger. She was ready to leave. He closed his eyes, and the moment, the final connection, simply ended.

I did not know I was witnessing the last moment of his life.

The formal news of his death arrived years later. I was in seventh grade. Mama walked into the kitchen, stated plainly, "Your daddy died," and continued on with whatever she was doing, her face a neutral, unreadable mask. She traveled to Memphis alone for the funeral. When she returned, it was just another Tuesday. There were no tears, no shared grief, no storytelling. Just the fact of a man who had left us—and in his wake, left behind a staggering $300,000. The money made us stable, but the fact of the inheritance was emotionally meaningless to me. I could not, and did not, connect the idea of financial provision to the reality of emotional presence. To me, he was just a dead guy who happened to have money.

Lisa, however, carried the full weight of his story. She remembered the constancy, the songs, the protection—the eight full years of safety I didn't share. And that memory became a torment. I do know that Lisa got the worst of life without a father. She lacked that essential emotional guard. I weep for that girl, not for what my father could have been, but for the chilling certainty of what was not done in his absence.

I learned that the single man Mama let in after my dad taught me to brace, to shield myself, to assume imminent harm. He stripped away any residual belief that a man was a natural protector. I wondered, even then, what my daddy would have thought of that: two young girls, growing up without a guard, existing in a home with no covering.

I stayed in my own marriage—through the hard, lonely, silent seasons—because I was obsessed with achieving the ideal I had never witnessed. I wanted my children to grow up with balance. With covering. With a love that was incapable of packing up and leaving without a word. I dedicated myself to the act of staying, not because I saw it modeled well, but because I saw, in the broken lives of my family, the terrible cost when no one stays at all.

His absence didn't just shape our childhoods; it irrevocably shaped the people we were forced to become.

Four

Six Months, An Eternity

The move that finally shattered the last, fragile illusion of my childhood innocence was the one that landed us on the Green Hill. We had physically progressed from the temporary, single-room rental—where my existence was a blur of roaches and the distant scent of Spanish—into a space we could actually call our own. This house, however, felt dense and heavy from the moment we crossed the threshold. It was painted a mossy, sickly green, and the cracked concrete stairway leading up to it felt impossibly steep to my short legs. I named it simply the Green Hill, a child's simple designation for what quickly became a deeply complex and utterly terrifying new beginning.

This period was still a collection of fragmented images, a kaleidoscope of sensory detail that never quite formed a continuous, stable narrative. I remember sitting on the cool linoleum floor, a bowl of soggy cereal clutched in my hands—my repeated ritual of postponed consumption. A few bites, then the irresistible pull to the world outside, where I'd run out barefoot, chasing an untainted sense of movement. I felt profoundly free in that external wildness, an innocence untouched by the shadows that were rapidly gathering force. But that external freedom was merely a defense mechanism, not a foundation.

That summer, the air itself seemed to hum with a nervous, unpredictable energy, a low-frequency hum that vibrated deep in my young bones. My sister, Lisa, went to live with our aunt in San Francisco.

It was meant to be a benign separation, a needed pause for her and Mama, but it became an eternity etched in acid onto the history of our family. Six months. A mere half-year, yet the trauma it held was monumental enough to redefine our genetic code.

When she came back, the girl I remembered—the playful, mischievous Lisa capable of spontaneous laughter—was gone, utterly erased. In her place was a whirlwind of pure, raw, uncontainable rage. She was impossibly grown, yet only ten years old. The transformation was so immediate and so jarring it was like witnessing a physical mutation. She argued with Mama with the savage, world-weary bitterness of a thirty-year-old woman, their voices clashing in the small house, creating a high-frequency tension that vibrated relentlessly through every room.

I was only five, barely having started kindergarten, and I possessed no framework for understanding the profound, abysmal horror that had transpired in those six months she was away. San Francisco didn't simply take her; something far more sinister, dark, and predatory had poisoned her essence. More truthfully, a vampire, disguised in the familiar skin of a family member, my aunt's husband, had systematically rewritten her very identity. He didn't just hurt her once; he employed physical violence, burning her, beating her, and showing her lessons of degradation that no child should ever be made to comprehend. He used poison and power, punishing every flicker of resistance, every failure to comply with his monstrous demands, until the child inside her was irrevocably extinguished.

My sister, the bright, curious child, died that year. Her body still breathed, her lungs still drew breath, but the essential light that had made her her—the boundless curiosity, the spontaneous laugh—was systematically erased. Six months of methodical torture had rewired her core into the terrifying, volatile stranger who returned. She came back irrevocably changed, a smoldering ember where a vibrant flame should have been. And in our quiet, structured home, no one—especially not my mother, who specialized in order, not emotional chaos—knew how to cool the devastating fire that raged within her.

The Vigilance of an Angel

The full, systemic horror of the abuse might have remained forever muffled by our family's pathological silence, if not for the intervention of a school counselor. This woman, a true angel in a landscape of shadows, noticed the tell-tale bruises littering Lisa's legs and refused to accept the easy lie that slipped from Lisa's mouth. This woman saw the truth that family was desperate to ignore. She pressed, gently but relentlessly, until the terrible truth—a jagged shard of glass—was forced out. The counselor, a tenacious advocate, made the call that physically brought Lisa home. God bless her, she rescued the body, but she could not save the soul.

Lisa's spirit was poisoned. Her soul, that fragile, violated vessel, was infected with a venom that destroyed her capacity for peace. My mother took her in, opening our home and providing the meticulous order she always relied on, but she had no idea—no map, no language—for how to heal a wound so fundamentally broken. And Lisa, shattered and without any safe space to process her torment, didn't know how to reconstruct herself.

The result was an immediate, consuming hatred between mother and daughter. The unspoken trauma created a battleground in our home. They fought loud, hard, violent wars that echoed through the house. Verbal bombs were detonated; doors were slammed with bone-rattling force, shredding the already fragile peace of our home. I, a tiny, small child, stood physically between them, a desperate mediator always trying to calm a turbulent sea I was far too small to navigate.

The sea never settled again.

The waves of pain grew louder, crashing relentlessly against the shores of our fragile family unit. The very air in our house seemed to grow perpetually thick, heavy with unspoken pain and rising tension. My mother, though physically present, began her slow, emotional retreat, her spirit fading like a photograph left too long in the sun. Her drinking returned—not a casual indulgence, but an insidious, waiting friend, always ready to offer a numbing balm against a reality too agonizing to confront. It was her version of turning off the light, of disappearing into the structural comfort of oblivion.

The Scars of the Mediator

My position became that of the tiny, anxious counselor. I was already reading the room, discerning the unspoken tensions, long before I had the words for it. I was stepping in, attempting to mediate the violent symphony of unresolved trauma that was their life. It was a burden far too heavy for a child's shoulders, yet I wore it out of necessity, out of a profound and desperate love for two people who were drowning.

Lisa wasn't just angry; she was starving. The venom the vampire had fed her in San Francisco had created an insatiable, psychic appetite—an emptiness she couldn't name, a wound no one helped her untangle. She had no language for her pain, no therapeutic room to process it, no clear exit from the torment. My mother, once a vibrant woman with dreams of becoming an actress, a singer, a star, saw those dreams fade a little more with each passing year. She used to dance around the house in Memphis, a picture of carefree joy. Now, she tiptoed through a silent, pervasive grief. The trauma had eclipsed her light.

It rained in our house for years. The walls stayed damp with unspoken rage, the air perpetually heavy with tension. I can't remember a single truly dry day, just the constant, suffocating humidity of fear.

This constant chaos, this psychic drowning, taught me everything about survival. We were all avid swimmers. Black kids in a world that often told Black people that water wasn't ours, that it was a realm of danger and exclusion. But my mother, with her characteristic defiance, made the water ours. She believed in diving, in the crucial, life-sustaining act of catching the second breath.

Lisa could stay underwater the longest, her lungs holding out for what felt like an eternity. I, however, always panicked. My lungs would burn, forcing me to break the surface too soon. I came up gasping, heart pounding. But perhaps that desperate, physical inability to hold my breath was the true lesson Mama had been teaching me all along.

It wasn't just how to swim, but how to survive the deeper, unseen currents of life. How to hold on when your grasp feels tenuous, when the weight of the world threatens to drag you under. How to find that elusive second breath—the one no one tells you exists, the one that emerges only when you've expended every ounce of your known capacity and think the drowning is certain. It has taken me a lifetime to understand its profound meaning. But I know now: the second breath always comes. And when it does—you don't just survive.

You rise.

Five

The Visit of the Vampire

The vampire visited my home long before my sister was sent to San Francisco, and like all plagues and generational traumas, he never truly left. He simply shifted forms, a constant, mutating shadow in our lives. I came to believe that the original vampire was an older family member who had been recently released from prison, someone who began systematically visiting violence and spiritual contamination upon the children in my extended family. Yet, this man was only a conduit; I knew, deep in my bones, that his instruction manual was derived from something far older and far darker.

I think back to those agonizing summers at my grandmother's house, those relentless periods where I waited for a father who never arrived. As we grew older, our games shifted, becoming unsettling moments that triggered a profound, internal sense of wrongness. You were a child, but you were 100% sure something was wrong—you just didn't have the sophisticated emotional or verbal tools to name it, to understand it, or to stop it. My earliest memories often feel like I was a powerless fly on the wall, observing a nightmare I was unable to halt, absorbing details I wouldn't wish upon any living soul.

Some of those summers, I vividly remember older cousins playing a grotesque game on my blind and deaf great-grandmother. She would sit quietly in the living room, a vulnerable, stationary fixture. I recall with chilling clarity older cousins exposing themselves, acting as if they would rub against her face. I don't remember my exact age, only the immediate, piercing certainty that this act was profoundly wrong. We younger cousins sat frozen, unable to move, unable to scream, united in a place of terrible silence. That enforced silence became the first, cruel lesson in survival: see everything, say nothing, and learn, instantly, how to disappear. The knowledge gained in that quiet corner was the knowledge of the powerless, the terrifying understanding that safety was found only in absolute stillness.

The breakdown was visibly active in my sister. Often, she would go into the back room with those older cousins, and we would hear her muffled screaming from the living room. Our childhood coping mechanism was terrifyingly simple: we would violently turn up the volume on the cartoons, desperately believing that if we didn't acknowledge the sound, the pain couldn't touch us. We were small children performing a terrifying, coordinated lie, acting out the ultimate lesson of generational trauma: what is not seen does not exist.

I think back to all these silent movements, these terrible, unspoken truths, and realize that the core of my fight was the realization that I didn't want to be silent. But being noisy wasn't the option either. My sister and mother chose to be loud: my sister with raw words and uncontrolled rage, my mother with her fists and her desperate need for structural order. Me, I chose a different battleground. I didn't scream wildly; I fought with educated and understanding words, words backed by faith. I chose to become the scholar of my own trauma.

Sexual abuse was not an isolated incident; it was a plague that infected our entire childhood environment, all of our homes, and for no possible justification. It shaped us all. The men in my family developed a profound, desperate need for psychological domination, driven by the physical pleasure of sexual exploration. Children were tragically easy targets because, once again, we had no voice, no experience, and no way to scream or stop what was happening. The endorphins released from an orgasm became, in their minds, proof of a perverse confidence and control. We were victims before we even understood the dictionary meaning of the word.

The Long Shadow of Silence

Of course, a child couldn't possibly understand the historical context of this trauma. It took decades of schooling, rigorous study, deep dives into history, relentless reflection, and desperate prayer to even find a language capable of processing it all. For years, the work of my adulthood was simply trying to find a name for the crushing, unnamed weight I carried, only to discover that the trauma's origin story was centuries old.

My sister's pain, particularly, haunts my work. She came to me in her late 30s, seeking help to write her story, to finally process the horrific images that had plagued her since she was small. Her script explicitly depicted the scene of a child learning to please a grown man—an uncle, a caregiver. The trauma was compounded by the family's reaction: my aunt claimed it was Lisa's fault, that she was "too mature for her age."

This despicable narrative of blame is the direct American legacy of sexualizing the young Black female at a very early age. When we move our hips and dance because we love the rhythm of the drum, it is instantly construed as an invitation to violation. Yet, when another culture's dancer performs the same motion, it is celebrated as cultural art. We are perceived as something to violate. The historical narrative of white women's jealousy provided a societal backdrop, but my sister, at eight, was incapable of posing any adult threat. How could her profound, innocent vulnerability not be protected or guarded?

I could never make my sister safe enough; no one could. And so, she turned to drugs, a desperate, chemical attempt to chemically erase the image from her mind. Her passing, though it broke my heart, has profoundly liberated my voice. There is no longer a need to shield her or the family secrets.

I believe that the original vampire's instruction manual was derived from the slave yards and the continuous pain visited upon my ancestors. Slavery, which so many in this country wish to simply for-get, systematically taught our families depravities that no one should ever endure. This is psychological warfare against our families. The institution deliberately separated families to demonstrate absolute control and power over our lives. Later, they hung our men, then im-prisoned our men. Then came the crack epidemic—a devastating, sys-temic disaster where drugs were supplied to our communities, and men went to prison or suffered addiction.

The silence we inherited was not merely a family secret; it was a psychological mechanism of survival passed down through blood-lines, ensuring that the deepest harm would never be discussed, let alone healed. How do we heal when we never acknowledge or deal with things out loud? This is why I hate silence, but I hate ignorance more. Not knowing and not wanting to know all seem like suppres-sion of a voice, of a freedom, of the American Dream. Sometimes I don't know how to put this into a society where every day someone walks by and you're supposed to say, "Hi, I am fine," because no one wants to hear all your pain. But what do we do with all the pain, all the trauma? Now, when people want to erase your history and your necessity, how do we heal when we haven't even dealt with the initial trauma of being an American citizen?

To me, America means dream and live out loud. Don't stay hidden.

This memoir, this unfiltered truth, is the final act of love and pro-tection I was unable to provide when we were children. Her scream-ing is finally heard through my pen. This is the provision of dignity that our family was never afforded.

Six

The Green Hill, The Gun, and The Cous

The aftermath of my sister's trauma, the profound, psychological destruction detailed in the preceding chapters, settled upon our lives like a toxic, permanent dust. The Green Hill house, where the initial terror of her return began, became a physical monument to our unhealed wounds. Though we had moved into this place of our own, hoping to build a fortress against external threats, the internal chaos of Lisa's rage and Mama's fear quickly tore through the walls. The constant, high-frequency tension that defined their relationship—the mother trying to impose order on the shattered daughter—was the only weather system we knew.

This tension soon manifested in a moment of terrifying, accidental violence. One day, while my mother was sitting calmly in the rocking chair talking on the phone, Lisa, still operating in a state of traumatized confusion, found a gun. The sound of the blast was instantaneous and sharp, ripping through the manufactured silence of the house. I remember the shocking stillness that followed. Mama didn't scream, didn't shout, or panic in the dramatic way a normal person would. She simply looked down at the sudden, blossoming red on her leg and stated flatly, with a chilling lack of emotion, "I think I've been shot." Her profound numbness—her ability to process an immediate, life-threatening injury as nothing more than a factual inconvenience—was infinitely more terrifying than any cry could have been. It was the ultimate expression of the silence at work: filling the huge, screaming gap where a normal reaction to pain should have been heard. Her response taught me that the internal world of the mind could become so chaotic that the external world, even a gunshot wound, was rendered insignificant. The self was already too heavily armored to feel the knife.

We moved across the street soon after, hoping the physical relocation would sever the trauma, but the heavier air of arguing and tension simply came with us, clinging like humidity. I spent hours outside, desperately riding my bike, chasing a peace that was always just beyond the perimeter of my vision. I was too young to fully name the profound anxiety, but I knew, instinctually and profoundly, that life wasn't supposed to feel like that. The brief, physical respite was soon followed by a resurgence of external danger. During a fight with a girl who followed Lisa home, my mother—all 4'11" and 90 pounds of fierce, protective resolve—stood like an immovable fortress in the doorway. She didn't flinch. Her body was small, but her presence became the wall, the absolute, final defense against the immediate, external threat. But that act only highlighted the terrible truth: there were things she simply could not block—the internalized violence, the quiet poison, the things we carried inside the walls that continued to tear us apart.

The years following Lisa's return were defined by my desperate need to mediate the constant domestic warfare. I was always stepping in, attempting to translate the rage of the abused daughter into something my mother's ordered mind could process, and trying to protect Lisa from the inevitable, harsh consequences of her fury. It was a burden far too heavy for a child's shoulders, yet I wore it out of a profound and desperate love for two people who were drowning. I was already reading the room, discerning the unspoken tensions, long before I had the words for it. I was becoming the anxious counselor and the unwanted peacemaker before I was even old enough to fully understand the concepts of trauma or forgiveness.

The Joyful Chaos of the Cousins

Then, a surprising burst of pure, chaotic light entered our lives when my Auntie Lina and her kids—my cousins Renee, Two, and G—moved in with us. Their arrival completely shifted the dynamics of our home. My mother's world was one of meticulous, labeled order—every drawer, every cupboard, every surface was governed by a military precision, her necessary defense mechanism against the chaos of her life. My cousins, by stark contrast, were joy let loose.

They were unrestrained laughter, daring rooftop jumping across the narrow alleys of Inglewood, and the shared, exhilarating thrill of ding-dong ditch. Their days were a beautiful, messy blend of life lived entirely on instinct. They were chaos, yes, but it was the kind of chaos I didn't know I desperately needed. They brought a raw, essential light and spontaneity into a home that had grown dim and heavy with fear and silence. They possessed an unburdened spirit I had long since lost.

That precious time, which spanned my third-grade year, remains one of the only full periods I remember feeling truly and completely like an unburdened kid. We jumped off porches like superheroes. We ate stolen pomegranates and corner store candy with sticky, joyous hands. We simply breathed without having to perform an act of emotional triage. But even in that pure, external joy, the internal war raged on. The house was constantly split between my mother's need for perfect order and my aunt's natural messiness. It was a silent war of conflicting coping mechanisms, and I stood in the middle, trying sometimes to organize the fighting, sometimes to simply disappear entirely.

The Arrival of Tim

The fragile peace shattered again when the calendar page turned and we moved back to the house on Hillsdale, the one near Centinela Hospital, coinciding with my fourth-grade year. It was here that my mother met Tim. He entered our lives subtly, in my third-grade year, but by fourth grade, he moved in. He was big, loud, angry, and eventually violently unpredictable. His presence was a pervasive, suffocating force that immediately brought the tension levels back to a breaking point. He was the return of the terror we had fled Memphis to escape, but this time, Mama had invited him in.

Mama, simultaneously, began drinking more, seeking solace and chemical escape in the bottom of a bottle. She worked tirelessly, relentlessly, providing for us, but she also disappeared more, her spirit retreating further behind a protective shield. Her perfectionist drive was now being fueled by alcohol and the need to maintain an ever more fragile façade. She was a perfectionist in every other aspect of her life—her home, her appearance, her work—but she had no capacity for emotions. We didn't talk about real things in the light of day. True feelings were reserved for the privacy of written words on paper, or buried deep within the structural recesses of closets.

Lisa, unable to cope with the unhealed wound and the crushing new presence of Tim, began carving out her own dangerous path of survival. She needed an escape, a sense of control where there was none. She started selling drugs. I remember her handing me a small, tightly packed bag once, her face serious, and telling me to hold it, promising me candy as a bribe. I did as I was told, clutching the illicit weight tightly, innocent and trusting. I didn't know until decades later what terrible, illicit weight I had carried in my small, unsuspecting hands.

The violence Tim brought was constant and escalating. The house was always damp with unspoken rage. I remember him grabbing Lisa by the neck on the stairs, lifting her like she was nothing. Mama watched. Said nothing. Her silence, again, was the loudest sound in the room. And I remember thinking, in a moment of cold, terrible acceptance: maybe that's just how it is.

We moved again to Hawthorne when I was in fifth grade. That beige, quiet house would become the one I finally called home, the foundation of my adolescence. But every single thing that preceded it—the green hill, the rocking chair, the gunshot, the daycare, the drugs, the stairs, the cousins, the secrets—those moments built me. They built me not cleanly, not gently, but fully. I carried it all: the soggy cereal and the bloody towel, my mother's terrifying stillness and my sister's consuming storm. I carried the weight, even when I didn't know it had a name. And this memoir, this act of speaking it fully, is the long, difficult process of finally learning to put some of it down.

Seven

The Hidden Gymnast

I used to fly. The memory of it is not a thought, but a visceral feeling—the precise, thrilling sensation of air rushing past my skin as gravity briefly conceded its hold. In fifth and sixth grade, when the chaos at home was reaching its most suffocating peaks, my body offered a profound counter-argument to my environment. I could execute four, five flips in a row. No hands. No hesitation. No fear. I could backbend until my world was upside down, handspring across any stretch of grass, and twist midair like a ribbon freed from its spool. Gymnastics wasn't something I ever formally trained for; it was an innate language my body already knew how to speak, a secret, effortless skill that manifested the moment my feet left the ground.

I wasn't the picture-perfect girl that the world casts as a gymnast. I was sturdy, muscular, and unapologetically a tomboy. I lacked the delicate, cultivated grace of the girls who were professionally trained. But when I moved, I felt utterly, completely free. I didn't know the word for it then, but I understand now that the feeling was pure liberation. For thirty seconds at a time, sometimes less, I wasn't the anxious little girl trapped inside a house thick with secrets and crushing silence. I was weightless. I was in command of my own trajectory. I was a moment of perfect, balanced order in a life that contained none.

The world outside the school walls became my improvised training ground. Oxford Elementary had these three beautiful, scarred steel bars on the playground—the kind built for challenging yourself, for hanging from, and for defying expectation. Those bars became my altar, the site of endless, desperate practice. But when we moved, and I transferred schools, those reliable structures disappeared. So, I improvised. I learned to flip off fences that were too high. I climbed trees whose limbs were too brittle. I used broken walls and sharp curbs as my balance beams. I actively, relentlessly turned my own body into a dynamic place of wonder, a mobile sanctuary that no one could take away or stain.

The true genius of this practice was its invisibility. No one at home knew. Not truly. My mother, consumed by her own battle with work and survival, didn't have the mental capacity to observe my triumphs. Lisa was perpetually checked out, floating in and out of the house in her own storm of trauma and rebellion. Tim was a constant, angry shadow. Gymnastics was never something anyone asked me about; it simply didn't fit into the suffocating architecture of our home life. But at school, the silence broke. The teachers noticed. The other kids watched. That recognition—that simple fact of being seen for my inherent talent—was oxygen. That's probably why I loved Oxford: not for the building, but for the precious, temporary space it gave me. It wasn't much, but it was mine, and it was real.

Back home, everything was constructed of brittle, enforced rigidity. The house was perpetually labeled, policed, and polished. My mother, the absolute perfectionist, maintained the illusion of control with terrifying meticulousness: drawers were alphabetized, closets were color-coded, and every jar and bottle was forced to face forward like soldiers on a store shelf. But inside that extreme physical order was a profound, wild kind of silence. We were incapable of speaking about anything real—the abuse, the fear, the anger, the boys who came and went in my sisters life, the constant threat of violence. We played. We laughed. But we didn't speak the truth. It was a trade-off: physical control for emotional silence. It was at Oxford that I started to write again, to move again, and to truly notice the sharp, painful distinction between my two lives.

The Fall and the Fear of Forgetting

The year I fell was the last time I truly flew. It wasn't a quiet moment of introspection; it was triggered by provocation. A girl, driven by a dull, casual cruelty, dared me—taunted me, really—saying I couldn't pull off my most complex flip combo again. I was confident, bordering on cocky, fueled by the conviction that my body was infallible. But as I landed, the moment dissolved. I don't remember the impact. The sequence—the flying, the execution, the shocking thud—is simply missing from my memory file. I just remember the cold, disorienting shock of waking up later in the nurse's office. They said I had a concussion.

I never flipped with that total, unrestrained freedom again. It wasn't because I became suddenly afraid of falling. The fear was deeper, more psychological: I was terrified that I didn't remember the fall. The loss of memory—the blank space between perfect flight and violent impact—haunted me. I couldn't rebuild the confidence if I couldn't recall the error. Losing control of the moment between absolute freedom and sudden violence was a trauma in itself, a chilling reminder that the world could strip away everything, even the memory of your own body's triumph.

Still, the instinct for movement stayed in my bones. The truth I understand now is that I was perpetually trying to outrun something—the silence, the shame, the looming threat of the unnameable chaos.

When my cousins, Auntie Lina's kids, came to live with us that year, the whole house tilted toward possibility. Renee, Jr, Rj—we were an inseparable knot of chaos and kinship. They didn't just come in; they broke the rigid mold of my mother's order. We jumped rooftops, stole pomegranates from neighbors' yards, and terrorized the block with endless games of ding-dong ditch. They were messy, loud, and gloriously, recklessly joyful. And I loved them fiercely for it.

They didn't know how much they truly saved me. It wasn't just that they were fun; it was that they were still kids, fundamentally untainted by the adults' paralysis. Even with the constant screaming, even when the adults were passed out or emotionally absent, my cousins refused to fold under the oppressive weight of our house. They ran through the trauma. They laughed through the fear. They played through the pain. They offered a critical, living lesson: you could still be wild, even when the world was desperately closing in.

And in those rare, precious moments—when I was flipping, or racing across a rooftop, or collapsing with laughter until my sides ached—I remembered, with piercing clarity, exactly who I was before the secrets began.

I remembered the girl before the vampire's shadow fell.

I remembered the girl before silence became a second language.

I was a gymnast. A writer. A small, resilient girl who used to fly.

Notes

Eight

Paper and a Flashlight

The morning began with a deceptive, almost cruel tranquility. I was just playing, entirely submerged in the serious business of childhood. Crawling along the carpet, I was a wild thing, humming a cartoon melody I liked, perfectly aligned with the rhythm of my own small universe.

The sun, a timid thing, was peeking through the window, soft and unsure, hesitant to commit fully to the day. It was the kind of light that hasn't decided yet if it wants to be gentle or loud.

My bowl of cereal, already half-finished, sat neglected on the floor. I never possessed the patience to finish it in one sitting; I'd eat a few bites, become utterly distracted by the overwhelming pull of play or thought, and leave it, always returning later to the soggy, comforting mush. I don't remember the specific layout of the apartment's furniture, only the absolute feeling of that morning. I remember the quality of the light, the sense of unearned safety, and what it felt like, for just a fleeting second, to feel profoundly normal.

We were living in Inglewood then, tucked into a small, one-bedroom apartment behind someone else's house. It was small, but Mama had made it a sanctuary—our private oasis. My mom, my sister, and I all shared the single bedroom. There was a twin-over-full bunk bed, and the coveted top bunk was mine—a small, physical perch of sovereignty. Our furniture, though simple, had purpose and style: a wide, white six-drawer dresser and a tall four-drawer chest nearby.

Our space wasn't themed with the cheerful noise of Disney princesses; it was painted purple, my favorite color then and now, chosen with Mama and Lisa's shared approval. There was a quiet harmony in that room, a consensus that suggested that despite the chaos outside, here, maybe, we were okay. Here, maybe, we could actively construct our own fragile peace.

Shattered.

It started with a slam. Loud. Sharp. It came from the front of the house and cut through the stillness of our morning like a blade through soft fruit. My small arms froze mid-movement. I blinked, startled, the sudden, terrible sound demanding my full attention. A second slam followed, louder, closer, the violence of the sound ratcheting up the tension in the space. Then, the voices: Tim's voice, booming and angry, a massive, uncontained wave of masculine rage. And then my mother's voice, rising immediately to meet it. She wasn't crying. She wasn't afraid.

She was screaming back, yelling with fire, refusing to back down.

I paused, still on all fours on the carpet, listening to the war escalating down the hallway. I didn't feel fear immediately. Instead, I felt a terrible, fierce sense of readiness. I felt ready to go fix it. That was the role I had been forced into, the one I had unwittingly claimed: I was the fixer. The brave one. The bold one. The one who could physically get between my mom and Lisa and force them to listen, to stop. I genuinely believed, with the arrogant confidence of a small child who has seen too much, that I could do the same now with Tim. I believed I had that kind of power, that my words and presence could tame a tempest. I did not yet understand that some storms are beyond reason, beyond negotiation, beyond my tiny influence.

I got up, moving silently, tiptoeing toward the hall. Every step was deliberate, like I was sneaking into a sacred, dangerous place I didn't belong but couldn't stay away from. I rounded the corner, still carrying the desperate, frantic hope that I might be the one to stop the escalating noise.

Extinguished the hope.

My mother. Five feet tall. Maybe 100 pounds soaking wet. Fierce and proud. Her voice was raised, her eyes wide and wild with defiance. She was not backing down.

And Tim.

Six-foot-four. Over 280 pounds. Towering. Angry. Brutal. A figure of absolute, terrifying physical superiority.

He punched her. Right in the face.

I had never seen that before. Not truly. I had heard the vague stories of my father's violence, the background noise of the past. But I had never seen a fist connect with my mother's face. Not like that. Not right in front of me. The sound didn't just hurt her; it cracked something deep inside me. Not like fragile glass—but like bone. Like something hard and foundational within my core sense of reality had suddenly snapped in half.

She stumbled, grabbing her face, her body suddenly losing its rigid posture. He shoved her down like she was nothing—a piece of laundry, a discarded object. And in that moment, the violence of the scene seized my body. I couldn't breathe. My feet, which had carried me toward the danger, stopped moving, rooted instantly to the floor. My voice—that defiant, strong voice that had been so ready to roar—vanished entirely. I couldn't speak. Couldn't yell. Couldn't fix it. The only reaction left was absence.

Frozen

And then, survival took over. I ran.

I didn't try to intervene again. I turned away from the hallway, away from the chaos, away from my mother and Tim and the unnameable violence. I ran straight into our bedroom. Past the bed. Past the chair. Straight to the closet.

I yanked the closet door open and scrambled inside, driven by a desperate, animal instinct for darkness and cover. It was pitch black. It smelled like old shoes, wood, and the faint, safe dust of things forgotten. I sank instantly to the bottom, curled into the tightest ball possible, my knees pulled to my chest, my forehead pressed hard against the cold, unyielding wall. My breath came out slow and shallow, a ragged, shaky rhythm. I didn't cry. Not yet. I simply focused every fiber of my being on the singular task of disappearing.

The yelling was louder now, closer, then farther. The sound of something slamming again—a wall, a body, perhaps both. I could hear my own heart beating, a frantic, trapped drum against the silence of the closet. I pressed deeper into the corner, wishing with a child's impossible faith that I could physically fold myself into nothingness.

Then, a flicker of memory, a life raft in the dark. My journal.

I scrambled out of the closet and grabbed it—pink, with a unicorn on the front, a ridiculous, perfect symbol of innocence and escape—from the dresser. My pen was somewhere nearby, and I found it. Back inside the closet I went. Door shut. Light off.

Flashlight.

Click.

That small, concentrated beam of light was everything. It sliced through the absolute darkness, and wherever the light touched, the space felt immediately safe. It felt like the chaos and the violence could not physically penetrate that glow. I don't remember the content of the words—maybe nothing rational, nothing that made sense to an outside observer—but I remember the profound physical and spiritual sensation. I was building a barrier. I was staking a claim, saying, "This is mine. You can't touch this part of me."

The pen moved fast, furiously. Not loops or doodles, but real words. Real sentences. I wrote about the paralyzing fear. About the fundamental incomprehension of why people hurt each other. About wishing for safety. About the desperate, aching need for someone—anyone—to truly see me, hidden in the dark. The words came like water finally breaking through a damn after years of pressure. My hand shook violently. My eyes blurred with unshed tears. I rocked gently, back and forth, a silent, necessary rhythm of self-soothing.

And then, something changed, something utterly outside of the logical world I knew.

There was a warmth. It was not the warmth of the flashlight bulb, or the confined air of the small space. It was something else entirely. Like arms wrapping around me, but without any physical touch. Like a profound, unshakeable peace that slid into the closet like smoke under a door. I didn't hear words in the way humans speak, but I felt a communication that was deep, quiet, and holy:

It's okay. I got you. You're not alone.

My shoulders dropped instantly, released from the paralyzing tension. My breath slowed, becoming deep and even. The tears finally came then—slowly at first, then faster, a cleansing torrent. I didn't bother to wipe them. I let them fall. I didn't want to move. Didn't want to leave. Didn't want to be anywhere else in the entire world.

That's where I met God.

Not in a church. Not in a pew. Not in a sermon delivered by a man.

In a closet. With paper. And a flashlight.

He wasn't just confined to that small closet. He showed me the world—my chaotic, shattered world—as if it were a snow globe resting safely in His hand. He was holding it. Holding me. And even though everything outside that tiny, wooden space was crashing and shattering, He whispered the unshakable truth that I was safe. That I mattered. That this moment, this trauma, would not be the thing that ultimately broke me.

I stayed in that closet for a long, necessary time. The scene outside kept spinning—yelling, crashing, the sound of violence repeating. But inside, it was still. Still and profoundly sacred. My permanent, chosen sanctuary.

After that day, the terror found new forms. I started having nightmares, not the simple kind where monsters chase you, but the clinical kind: sleep paralysis. Visions where my body would wake up, but my voice wouldn't follow. My eyes would be open, but I couldn't move. Witches, shadows, and the echoing resonance of Tim's angry voice filled the room. I had no words for it, no one to tell. So, I returned to the pen. I wrote more. Scribbled in notebooks. Doodled on napkins. Kept the most dangerous secrets safely contained within the pages.

I learned to trust that hiding wasn't weakness—it was profound wisdom. It was a strategy of protection. It was knowing that not every battle needed to be fought out loud or in public. That sometimes, the bravest, most essential thing you could do was survive quietly.

That closet became my central symbol. Not of fear, but of choice. Of claiming peace in the center of the storm. Of claiming a physical space for myself when no one else knew I needed one. It taught me to listen before speaking.

To feel before reacting. It taught me that the pen in my hand was power. And I started to believe—deep in my bones, with the certainty of revelation—that God gave me that power for a reason. That I would write. And through my writing, I would reach other little girls hiding in closets—real or metaphorical. That I would be their voice until they found their own.

Even when I became a teacher, I carried that sacred moment with me. I taught like every child might be hiding something. I gave voice to silence. I built confidence where shame used to sit. Because I never forgot what it felt like to have no words and too many feelings. I never forgot what it felt like to need light in the dark.

And I never will. God didn't just meet me there. He stayed.

And ever since, when the world gets too loud—when things crash and slam and break—I still
instinctively go back.

To the quiet.

To the pen.

To the page.

To the light.

Nine

The Girl Who Sang Better Than Whitne

I think I was firmly in my fourth-grade year when the accident occurred. I know this because the events of that afternoon were so
thoroughly intertwined with my sister Lisa's final withdrawal from
my orbit. She was supposed to walk me home from school that day, a
commitment that felt massive and sacred to my nine-year-old self,
and she simply never did. Lisa was five years my senior in age, but
truly, she felt like five lifetimes ahead in experience. Her world had
completely shed the simple concerns of spelling tests and kickball
games. Her orbit was entirely different, now revolving around boys
thick with cheap cologne, the secrecy of smoky basements, borrowed
perfume that reeked of musk and teenage rebellion, and stolen glances
that promised danger. She floated in and out of the house like some
kind of transient, mysterious grown woman—a fleeting presence
with no curfew, no apologies given or expected, carrying only the
heat of summer days and the thump of distant music and new, heavy
secrets always clinging to her breath.

That specific afternoon played out like a familiar, predictable film.
Lisa got home well before me, her footsteps quicker, her urgency driven by a purpose entirely separate from mine. But she wasn't rushing home to wait for me. She arrived, slipped in with some boy, their
laughter muffled by the quick closing of the door, followed by the def-

inite, intentional click of the lock, sealing the entire world behind them. She left me outside, just like that, with the cold finality of an afterthought. It was as if the small girl walking home slowly on the cracked pavement didn't exist, as if I weren't her sister at all.

And honestly? I didn't register the initial feeling as true abandonment. Not yet. I was the kind of solitary kid who possessed the ability to make an entire playground out of anything—a cracked sidewalk, the lonely iron lamppost, a patch of stubborn, sun-baked weeds. I had my skateboard, my well-worn, scuffed companion, which felt like a true extension of my will. The wind was my only reliable friend, a constant force pushing me forward, whispering silent stories in my ears. The rough concrete became my stage, ready for any trick or gravity-defying turn. I could get completely lost in my practice, over and over again, until my entire mind was dedicated to the precise mastery of a trick. My feet constantly itched to move, to feel the vibration of the wheels beneath them, and my head was always full of songs and elaborate, made-up stories. I could entertain myself for hours with nothing but a broken stick and a patch of dry, sun-baked grass.

My own internal world was vast, big, and utterly boundless.

Snap!

But then it happened. The sound, the bone-jarring jolt, the sudden, sharp, terrible feeling that sliced through my private world.

The owner's grandson—or perhaps his son, I never settled on his exact connection to the house—called my name from across the yard. His voice was bright, full of distracting, boyish energy. He was cute, that kind of cute you're technically not supposed to notice at nine years old, because boys are generally bothersome things, but you notice anyway. My head turned instinctively, a small, shy smile touching my lips. My braids swished across my shoulder, a sudden, minor distraction. And in that tiny, fatal moment of distraction, my foot wobbled just slightly on the board.

My skateboard, that trusted extension of my will, turned violently off course. I hit the unyielding brick wall of the house full speed, the thud echoing through the entire complex.

Pain.

That's the clinical word that comes to mind, still. But it is not enough. It wasn't just pain—it was pure, raw, instantaneous shock. My entire body jolted like it had been suddenly unplugged from the sun, every ounce of kinetic energy draining out of me in an instant. My knees gave out beneath me, sending me tumbling. My left arm hit the ground first, twisting unnaturally beneath me as I collapsed. A sick, wrong sound tore through the air. I didn't just hear it; I felt it, a grinding, tearing deep inside the bone. Snap!

I ran. Not calmly, not with the grace of the gymnast I secretly was, but with desperate, frantic energy. My legs were limping, my steps uneven and charged with adrenaline. I was shouting, a ragged, broken sound I didn't recognize as my own voice. I was dragging one arm, holding it strangely against my body, like it didn't belong to me anymore, like a foreign, hostile object. I stumbled and charged up the steps to our one-bedroom apartment, the little place perched behind the main house. It was small, but it was always full—full of memories, full of tension, full of a fierce, complicated love, and full of history that weighed heavy in the air.

I pounded on the door. My good hand, my right hand, hammering relentlessly against the unforgiving wood. "Lisa!" I screamed, my voice raw, torn between the agony of the pain and the desperation of the abandonment. I screamed for my sister to open the door, my pleas escalating from demanding to begging. I cried. I begged. I knocked until the skin on my knuckles went raw and bruised. My injured arm was held tight to my chest; I couldn't raise it. It felt like it was buzzing, vibrating with a loud, unwelcome energy—like the pain was hosting a party without me, and I was trapped outside its noisy perimeter.

Stillness Was Safety

I waited.

But she never came.

She and that boy? They were sealed inside, existing in another world entirely. A world filled with the distant, thumping bass of music, the soft, private sound of whispering mouths, and the definitive, cruel click of a locked bedroom door. They weren't thinking about me, the small, desperate sister crumpled on the steps, hurting. I was utterly invisible to them.

I sank down onto the concrete steps, the cool surface offering a brief, almost insulting comfort against the throbbing heat of my arm. I curled into myself, desperately trying to make my body small, holding my broken arm with my other hand as if it might float away, like a balloon on a string about to be lost forever. I cried until the tears finally dried up, leaving salty, stinging tracks on my cheeks. Until the intense sobbing gave way to little hiccups, small, shaky tremors that wracked my body.

Then, in that quiet, excruciating stillness, a profound realization emerged—a cold, clear, undeniable truth: If I didn't move it, it didn't hurt as much.

Stillness was safety. Stillness was medicine. It was a lesson learned through brute force, a survival tactic I would internalize and carry for years to come.

So I sat still. I clamped my mouth shut against any further sounds of distress, refusing to give the pain another victory. I held my arm like it was a precious, fragile sculpture—a broken one, yes, one you couldn't possibly fix with clumsy, frantic hands, but one you could still love if you simply didn't touch it, if you kept it perfectly, carefully, undisturbed.

And I waited.

I must have sat there for over an hour, maybe longer. Long enough for the harsh sunlight to yield to the fading orange of dusk. Long enough to watch a determined line of ants crawl across the step and trace the sticky, black lines of old gum stuck under the railing. Long enough to wonder, with a chill of terrifying clarity, if I was actually invisible. If maybe this was just how things worked when you were the little sister, the ancillary character often left to fend for herself against the violent unpredictability of the world.

Around 4:15 PM, a sound finally broke the silence. The front door cracked open, just a sliver of light. My sister, Lisa, peered out, her face still carrying the residual haze of her secret world. Her eyes landed on me, then drifted down to my arm, hanging at that impossibly unnatural angle. There were no gasps. No rushing. No frantic "What happened?!" Just a long, unblinking glance. A quiet, detached assessment. Then, she simply opened the door wider.

She let me in.

I walked straight past her, not saying a single word, my gaze fixed forward. I didn't even look at the boy she'd been with, his presence immediately becoming a forgotten detail in the face of my own consuming pain. I went straight to the dresser and pulled out a scarf. I have no memory of knowing what to do. I'd never seen a broken arm before, never seen anyone fashion a sling in real life. But the idea just clicked. My body, operating on a primitive, internal guidance system, told me exactly what it needed. I wrapped the scarf carefully, precisely, around my injured arm, creating a stiff, makeshift sling.

And I listened.

That simple, painful act of supporting it, of giving the limb a place to rest, solidified the awful truth: it was broken. Truly broken.

When my mom got home at 4:30 PM, her car pulling into the driveway with its familiar rumble, the mask of her emotional control shattered instantly. Her face changed the second her eyes landed on me, on the scarf-suspended arm. There was no hesitation, no questioning. She scooped me up with a mama's fury, a fierce, protective energy I rarely saw directed at simple injury, and we went straight to Centinela Hospital.

The Payback of the Easter Bunny

My broken arm was a heavy cast, a white, plaster reminder of Lisa's abandonment. But for me, the injury wasn't just a physical wound; it was an emotional account that had to be balanced, not with anger, but with the specific, annoying intensity of my little sister love. My way of expressing hurt was never direct conflict; it was always through a calculated, theatrical payback by love.

I decided I would torment Lisa with my presence, turning my injury into a badge of honor and a symbol of her carelessness. I found my vengeance in the one place I always created perfect order: my wardrobe. I had recently finished sewing a full outfit, a labor of meticulous craft and care. It was a chaotic masterpiece mixed entirely of my mother's black and white scraps—a patchworked, multi-patterned dress with a bright, crisp collar. It was my favorite creation, something I loved deeply because it was entirely my own work.

I decided this outfit was going to be my armor for a solid week.

With my sling holding my plaster arm, I marched out in my patchwork creation, hopped on my bike, and committed myself to a relentless, seven-day performance. My chosen soundtrack was pure, sugary absurdity: I rode my bike straight through the neighborhood, my voice soaring, singing "The Easter Bunny is Coming Home Today, The Easter Bunny!" I sang it over and over, all day long, day after day. The song was wildly out of season, wildly annoying, and performed with a total lack of shame. It was a glorious, calculated cacophony aimed directly at my sister's nerves.

The intended target, Lisa, could only respond with a mixture of raw laughter and profound frustration. But the greatest witness to my performance was her best friend, Tosha. Tosha had a voice that could genuinely sing circles around Whitney Houston—a true, undeniable gift that deserved a spotlight. She watched me, this uncoordinated, cycling, sling-wearing kid, singing off-key about the Easter Bunny, and she couldn't stop herself. Tosha laughed until she cried, collapsing in fits of hysterics every time I wheeled by. She cried because the performance was so ridiculous, so utterly me, and so completely effective.

That was the heart of my complex relationship with Lisa: she would do something careless, stupid, or terribly hurtful, and I would love her to death with my little-sister annoyances. It was the only way I knew how to process our pain—by turning it into absurd, shared joy, forcing a moment of laughter where there should have been only tears. We still cry so hard every time we think about this moment now, decades later. It's the perfect snapshot of a love that was forged in chaos and expressed in calculated, hilarious annoyance.

My sisterly love was loud, relentless, and impossible to ignore. And for one week, the entire neighborhood was subjected to my off-key tribute, all because my sister chose a boy over me on a single afternoon. The girl who learned stillness as survival was learning that sometimes, the greatest survival requires making the biggest, most absurd noise.

Interlude: Where Things Get Fixed

I swear, even though I was still throbbing with pain, a small, quiet part of me was... calm. Deeply, surprisingly calm. Because I loved that hospital.

It took me years to truly realize it, but the hospital—Centinela—was the second place I ever felt safe. Not safe like padded walls or bubble wrap, a superficial kind of protection. Safe like stillness. Like precision. Like everything made sense. Like someone smarter, stronger, and prepared was definitively in charge of making things right. It wasn't as deep, as sacred, as what I felt in the closet where God held me perfectly still—that was an otherworldly, divine embrace.

But this was close.

Hospitals had order. Charts were meticulously kept. Schedules were precisely followed. Machines hummed and beeped with the profound sound of purpose, relaying vital, factual information. Here were people who knew exactly what to do when bodies broke and things went terribly wrong. The world outside might be spinning, loud and sloppy and chaotic, but inside those antiseptic walls, there was a profound, reassuring calm. Stillness. Solutions.

Even the pervasive smell—sterile and sharp, a scent of antiseptic and clean linen—was comforting, a scent of competence. My mom belonged there. She moved through those halls like she mattered, her small frame radiating authority and concern. And because of her, because she was there, I mattered too, and that was everything.

Looking back, I think that's when I started falling in love with places that fix things. Places that hold chaos in one hand and healing in the other, without flinching. Places that don't shy away from what's broken, but lean into it with knowledge and purpose.

Maybe that's what I wanted to become. Not just a doctor. Not just a writer. But a place. A person who fixes what can be saved, who offers precision and care, and who holds what can't be fixed with compassion and understanding.

Even then, I understood something people don't always say out loud: little girls need saving in all kinds of ways. Not just from monsters or accidents. Sometimes from the silence that swallows screams. Sometimes from being overlooked, from feeling invisible. Sometimes from having to figure it all out by themselves, when they're too young to know how.

And titles don't mean anything to trauma. Not "Mom." Not "Sister." Not "Doctor." What matters is peace. What matters is care. What matters is knowing someone sees you. Someone holds space for you. Someone fixes what can be fixed—and stays with you through what can't.

That night, with my arm finally stabilized in a proper sling and my mom finally truly present and home, I didn't just feel physically better. I felt seen. I felt safe. And for a little girl who'd already learned how to hide, how to be still to survive, that feeling of being seen and safe was everything.

Ten

The House and The Mask

Hawthorne was the first physical space that ever felt genuinely, irrevocably mine. It was more than a mere address change; it felt like I had finally stepped into a room where a light had been deliberately left on just for me. Not a harsh, demanding glare, but a soft, steady, persistent glow. It was a quiet hum that settled deep in my bones, a sensation of peace I had never known. It felt like a breath held for far too long, finally, completely released—a slow, quiet sigh from the earth itself acknowledging my profound need for rest and stability.

We moved there when I was in seventh grade. The air itself carried a different promise, smelling not of car exhaust and old dust, but of damp earth after a rain, hinting at growth and possibility. The house itself was unassuming—beige walls with dark brown trim, a simple, non-threatening uniform against the sparse green lawn. It sat on a street that felt quieter than the ones we'd fled, not a dead quiet, but a gentle, respectful hush. Everything seemed muted. It wasn't perfect; nothing in our world ever was. But it was solid. It was built firm. It felt like the kind of place where roots might actually take hold, might grow deep into the ground without fear of being instantly ripped out.

For the very first time in my life, the act of unpacking my boxes was a deliberate, ceremonial process. I unfolded clothes slowly. I carefully arranged books on shelves. I placed trinkets and personal effects as if they mattered, as if they were fragile evidence of a life worth protecting. This was the first time I felt that possibility: a profound, quiet sense of permanence, of settling. A small, fragile hope blooming in my chest, a hope I was now strong enough to guard.

The Architecture of Courage

School, by contrast, remained a strategy. I was smart, quick-minded, and capable of acing any test without trying too hard. But I played my intelligence down. I'd already internalized the most brutal lesson of chaos: never shine too bright. Brightness drew attention, and attention always, inevitably, drew trouble. I wanted to blend perfectly, to become an indistinguishable part of the background hum. My primary goal was to coast through the days, through each class, through each hallway, and emerge from every moment entirely in one piece.

Yet, this stability allowed a new self to emerge. I began to actively like my life and the small world I was building. I found friends in Hawthorne. Real friends—who laughed easily and talked about gloriously silly, unimportant things like boys, clothes, and pop songs. I honed my natural defense mechanism: I was funny. I knew precisely how to crack a joke that eased the tension in a room, if only for a second. I learned to perform, using good grades and quiet politeness to charm my way into safe spaces: clubs where my mind could wander freely, and church, a place of comforting rituals and hushed promises. I was coming out of my shell not merely to socialize, but to fight for the life I wanted.

I became a master observer. I watched people more than I spoke to them, studying the minutiae of their faces, their easy, unburdened laughs. I studied the shifts in the atmosphere. The way bodies moved. The unspoken rules that governed their safe, uncomplicated world. I knew how to read a room like it was a secret language. I learned precisely when to become invisible, how to pull myself inward until I was nothing more than a ghost—unseen, unheard, untouchable. I was a spy in the kingdom of normalcy, ready to defend my small patch of peace.

The Shadow in the Sanctuary

But the threat was portable. Tim came with us to Hawthorne. His presence was a dark, suffocating cloud clinging to our new, quiet house, a shadow that lengthened and grew darker with every setting sun. This quiet period forced me to constantly hold the boundary against his sustained, insidious intrusion.

At first, the violation was small, subtle, disguised. Just comments. Words that slid under my skin like splinters—about my clothes, about my developing body, about my hair. They were always a little too close, a little too personal, meticulously disguised as jokes or casual observations. But they left a bitter, unmistakable taste—a cold, metallic tang of poison on my tongue.

Then came the "accidental" brushes. A hand brushing my back in the hallway, lingering a second too long. A hip bumping mine in the kitchen, a warmth that felt inexplicably cold and violating. A squeeze of my shoulder that wasn't comforting, but possessive. Each touch was a small, insidious violation. The worst part was the casual nature of it, the way he made it seem normal, making me doubt the sudden shivers that ran down my spine. It forced me to question my own reality, making me wonder if I was imagining the primal urge to shrink and vanish entirely.

I learned to disappear inside my body. My own skin ceased to be a home; it became a cage, a place of last resort to hide. I could be physically present in the room, standing right there in his line of sight, but be nowhere at all. My mind would simply float away, completely detach from the physical self. I would observe from a vast distance, like watching a poorly lit movie of my own life. I could see my hands. I could hear his voice. But I could feel nothing. I could be nothing.

This was the mastery of the mask: the blank stare, the quiet, compliant nod, the terrifying absence in my eyes, the fixed, unseeing smile. It was safer there, in the hollow, untouchable space behind my eyes.

The Drowning of the Adults

Around me, the house was drowning, even in its quiet state. Lisa was still spiraling, a wild, uncontrolled force. The abuse she suffered had fundamentally twisted her, and she was always searching for an external escape. Mama drank more. The bottles became a more constant presence, hidden in cupboards, under sinks. She worked tirelessly, but her mind was somewhere else entirely. She fought with Lisa in fierce, brutal wars that violently shook the walls. Their voices were sharp knives, cutting through the quiet house. And Mama slept too hard, a heavy, exhausted sleep that seemed to pull her into a different, unreachable world.

Some nights, I would stand watching her sleep, leaning close, holding my breath, terrified that she might stop breathing altogether—that she might choose to leave me too. Other nights, a desperate, quiet wish formed in my throat: that she would truly wake up. That she would finally, finally notice me. Notice the heavy silence I carried. The mask I wore. The struggle raging in my own small space. The little girl who was now building strength to fight back.

And I wrote. Always. The pen became a permanent, constant fixture in my hand. Journals filled with the questions I didn't know how to ask out loud, questions that burned in my mind like hot coals. The words were a direct, uninterrupted line from my soul to the paper. I was meticulously building something vital with those words: a fortress. A bridge. My own future. The pen became my quiet confidant. The paper, my only witness. It was the only space where I could scream without making a sound, the only place I could be truly, terrifyingly seen.

This period of stability in Hawthorne allowed me to cultivate the quiet strength I would soon need. The small space I carved out for myself—in the classroom, with my friends, in the pages of my journal—was not just survival. It was preparation. I was finding the courage to fight not just for peace, but for the right to exist unviolated. The house gave me the ground; my courage gave me the fight.

Eleven

The Silent Confrontation

The move to Hawthorne in my fifth-grade year marked a physical shift toward stability, but the quiet parts of our lives remained shattered—a silent, gaping wound that money couldn't mend. My mother was working as an accountant at a hospital, her days filled with the sterile smells and precise logic of numbers. Tim, a truck driver, was frequently on the road, yet his oppressive presence felt perpetually looming, a dark cloud clinging even in his absence. We were no longer poor in money, but we were desperately impoverished in emotional safety.

In fifth grade, the external world offered fragmented moments of grace. I remember a specific afternoon playing hide-and-go-seek with the boys in the neighborhood. The sun was warm on my skin, the air thick with the scent of cut grass. My friends, though just kids, seemed to possess an instinctive awareness of the hidden dangers in the world. "Don't let him do that," they'd whisper, their voices quiet but urgent, pulling me away from the edge of things I didn't fully comprehend. They acted as a silent shield, protecting me from shadows I couldn't yet see, their quick glances and small hands reinforcing the boundary I was learning to draw.

The Architect of a Lie

My mother's love, though fierce and profound, was a distant, steady hum. She was kind, always encouraging my grades and efforts, but her love was not communicated through shared secrets or long, intimate talks. Her own spirit, burdened by pain and her need to maintain the perfectionist illusion, lacked the capacity to truly know the girl hiding behind the mask. I wonder, even now—did she know the girl who felt too much and said too little? Was I merely the fragile hope she had left, a desperate prayer sent into the universe that I would turn out okay?

My room in Hawthorne became a physical metaphor for the contradiction I lived. It was a soft, comforting purple, with pale lavender walls and delicate, white lace curtains billowing gently with the breeze. These were my favorite colors then—purple, the color of dreams, and anything frilly, anything that felt soft and pretty. In my innocent mind, that room was a sanctuary, meant to be cute and safe. Yet, in my adult mind, I know it was a deliberate lie. It was a pretty cover over the pain, a deceptive sweetness designed to mask the lingering shadow of the vampire's trauma that was hidden beneath the ribbons and the lace.

The stability of Hawthorne, ironically, made the escalating danger of Tim more palpable. The routine of coming home became a slow-motion dread. The casual nature of his advances was the most insidious torture: small gestures that felt like a twisted kind of family fun, until the wrestling changed. It became me sitting on his lap while we watched TV. That seemed simple enough in my innocent mind. Innocent. Until it wasn't.

The Violation

The shift from simple physical closeness to absolute violation was chillingly slow. It went further. His fingers, a slow, deliberate crawl. It was a heavy weight. A silent, terrifying invasion of my innermost space. I thought it was just odd, a strange, unsettling warmth, but my body's defense mechanisms were already locking down. My physical self froze. I didn't know how to speak, how to scream, or how to move the hands that had once been so bold.

The realization that my body had locked down in a familiar, paralyzing freeze response—the same one that seized me when Tim punched my mother in Chapter 7—was a terrifying epiphany.

The script flipped.

I still say to this day—that's when I found my voice. The true one. The one that protected.

It never went past that specific violation because I stopped it. I didn't even know I was capable of stopping it. I didn't have a practiced argument or a plan. The words just came, raw and unfiltered, pushed out by a primal, absolute certainty of wrongness. I just said what I felt, what I knew was wrong. I told him, instantly recalling the shared legacy of pain, about the earlier violation by my cousin. I told him, my voice steady despite the tremor in my soul, "I don't like that. I like being your friend and I like playing with you—but not like that. That's not what I want. If you want to be friends, we can, but don't touch me like that."

The Birth of Hatred

And just like that, it stopped. His hand withdrew. The air shifted, the dense tension immediately replaced by a vacuum of cold absence. A fragile, terrifying victory.

But everything else stopped too. The playing. The wrestling. The casual questions about my day. The breakfast he sometimes made. The truce was over. The punishment for my courage was the silence—a cold, heavy blanket of emotional isolation that replaced the physical violence.

And it made me profoundly, righteously angry. A deep, burning rage that settled in my core. I yelled at him. I cursed at him. Every chance I got. People might have dismissed it as simple teenage rebellion, hormones, or misplaced attitude. But it wasn't. It was my inner four-year-old screaming. The one who had roared in the kitchen, amplified by the pain of every silent witness.

How dare you hurt my mom? My sister? And now me? Why do you still get to be here? Why do you still get to breathe in our home?

I cursed a lot. It started as a quiet habit, but it exploded then. A torrent of raw, defiant words. I still say: a profane world deserves a profane response.

My mother and Tim fought more and more, their battles escalating, fueled by her drinking, his rage, and the unspoken tension in the house. She was 4'11", 90 pounds. A tiny, fierce woman. He was 6'2", 300 pounds. A towering, brutal force. I was strong, 5'5", 120 pounds, with a muscular build forged from climbing and running—my body was a weapon I was learning to control. But I learned to only argue with him when she was gone, because I knew she would bear the brunt of his transferred rage. When she was safely away, I let him have it. I spoke freely. My words were sharp daggers, fueled by my singular, newly crystallized hatred.

This hatred was different. It was not the simple dislike of an abusive man. It was the absolute, final realization that he hurt my mom, he touched me, and I started to think he hurt my sister also. The thought that this man, who had violated me, may have also been complicit in the continued trauma of my already shattered sister, crystallized my rage. I hated him more profoundly than I ever could any other man because he was the continuation, the physical manifestation of the Vampire.

The Armor of the Word and the Body

This period—where I learned that speaking the truth had a price, but was mandatory—was the forge for my adult self. I stopped arguing with him when Mama was around because I knew she would pay for it: with her eyes, with her body, with her silence. So, when she was gone, I let him have it.

I wrote about my pain, spilling secrets onto pages, but I was largely silent in the external world, hiding behind my witty humor—a quick defense mechanism. I realized my body was a fortress. I loved health, weights, and athletics. My body was a weapon I controlled. I was physically strong, sharp with my words, a verbal sparring partner when required. But that was just defense. I was still lost inside, searching for the true map of myself.

I started to read a lot. I wrote a lot. Books became my shelter, their pages a refuge. Stories became my way out—portals to other worlds, other lives. That's when the deepest knowledge set in: I wanted to be a writer. A film director. I wanted to tell and direct stories like mine, to shine a light on the hidden corners, so people could understand. So no one else would feel invisible.

This period was the beginning of my true voice, my courage, and my words becoming my armor, my shield, my weapon. The long, winding road ahead was clear: I had to survive this house, and then I had to go speak the truth of what happened in the silence.

Twelve

Middle School Beginnings

Middle school arrived as a sudden, strange, and utterly necessary gift. It appeared in the narrative of my life as a perfect, small bubble in time, a quiet, unexpected space where I finally started to feel like I belonged to something beyond the suffocating confines of our house in Hawthorne. I needed desperately to belong to something beyond its creaking floors, its heavy, unspoken silences, and the perpetual shadow of Tim's anger. That external world—the hallways, the gym, the cafeteria—became my crucial, vibrant tether to normalcy and sanity.

I continued to invest energy in controlled, reliable outlets. I still played in the band, the loud, brassy sound of my saxophone a defiant, joyful noise that actively worked to drown out the low, constant hum of home tension. I loved the feeling of basketball—the rhythmic thump of the ball against the asphalt, the squeak of my sneakers on the court—finding solace in the controlled aggression of sport. Yet, the lack of an official team didn't matter. Something bigger and more essential was happening: I was about to find my best friend, the single most significant lifeline of my adolescence.

In seventh grade, I was, by nature, quiet and strategically guarded. I had acquaintances, kids I sat with at lunch, but fostering genuine friendship was impossible when the internal noise of my home was always louder than the school bells or the hallway chatter. It was simply too hard to let anyone in, to expose the fragile cracks in the foundation I was trying so desperately to hide.

The Simpson's Shirt and the Unfiltered Truth

Then, I met Alisha.

The very first day we truly spoke was defined by a moment of startling, accidental honesty—a moment that ripped through the polite social fabric of middle school. I was wearing a brightly colored Simpsons T-shirt. My maiden name was Simpson, a fact that had always been an easy target for teasing; my response was to fiercely lean into the mockery, reclaiming the name and wearing the clothes as armor.

That day, Alisha, with her quick, sharp eyes and even sharper wit, zeroed in on the image. She teased me about the Marge shirt, pointing out how the towering blue hair of the cartoon character was stretched across my chest, distorted by the fabric. It was a typical middle school taunt, but instead of shrinking, I met her gaze with my inner four-year-old's defiance. There was no flinching. My voice, steady and calm despite the suddenness of the interaction, delivered a raw, unfiltered fact: "That's because I have big breasts. They do that."

She froze for a stunned second, processing the sheer audacity of my statement. Then, she released an immediate, visceral torrent of laughter—a full, unrestrained, joyful sound that echoed through the crowded hallway. Her head thrown back, her shoulders shaking. Just like that, in the space of a single, powerful sentence that asserted a physical fact and reclaimed my power, we became best friends.

The connection was instantaneous and profound. We became inseparable, joined at the hip. I finally had a friend—a real one—who knew my life, who knew my home, not all the deepest scars, but enough to understand the dark shadows I was running from.

The Second Sanctuary

Alisha's home became my second, crucial sanctuary. Her mother was young, vibrant, and incredibly accessible. In stark contrast to the emotional rigidity and perfectionism of my own home, their house was open. Not just the physical door, but the very air inside was open and

breathable. Words were said out loud, questions were welcomed, and genuine emotions were allowed to exist without fear of consequence. There were no silent, festering secrets hidden in the corners. It was bizarrely unfamiliar to me, yet simultaneously beautiful and free.

Alisha and I lived about five miles apart, a distance that felt vast and endless to middle school legs, yet we walked to each other's houses every single day, the physical distance a small price to pay for emotional safety. I rode my bike, my skates, my skateboard—whatever got me there faster. Alisha's mom, with her cool wisdom, always made us meet in the middle, a small, yet significant act of protection that ensured we weren't walking alone in the encroaching dangers of the city. We would stay late into the night, the hours blurring as we simply talked, laughed, and dreamed.

We were a profound study in contrasts. Alisha was tall, skinny, dark-skinned, beautiful, and unapologetically girly. She wore bright colors, and her hair was always perfect. I was her opposite: a tomboy, light-skinned, already tall at 5'5", with a muscular build. But I had already started hiding my body. My chest was developing, drawing an unwanted, new kind of gaze that made my skin crawl and triggered the defensive instincts learned in Tim's shadow. I started wearing baggy hoodies and loose jeans—anything to obscure my shape. I desperately wanted to be invisible again, even as my personality demanded attention. The constant balancing act between the desire to be seen and the need to be safe was exhausting.

The Voice on the Page

Middle school was the stage where my voice, once a terrifying roar in the kitchen, began its transition into a disciplined, literary weapon. I wasn't defined by the "cool kids," but Alisha and I were cool with everyone, moving between groups easily. We laughed constantly, a joyful noise that actively worked to fill the empty, silent spaces inside me.

And I started getting into trouble—for writing.

In English class, the words simply poured out of me, a torrential overflow of thoughts and observations filling pages. My grammar was often a messy tangle, but my stories held a raw, undeniable power. My teacher, Mrs. Cole, was the first adult outside of my private journal to truly affirm this capacity. Her eyes would light up when she read my messy pages, and she affirmed my voice, recognizing that it mattered.

In history class, my defiance found a political edge. I got into trouble constantly because the textbook versions of race—Black and white issues—felt flat, incomplete, and fundamentally dishonest. I simply could not stay quiet. My voice, once a small, defiant roar, was now finding its power through education and the fierce desire for truth.

My writing, my courage, and my words were becoming my intellectual armor, my shield, my weapon. I had a life outside of home now—a place to breathe, a place to be seen. That external world was a vital lifeline, allowing me to build the inner strength I needed for the difficult final years at home, and the massive confrontation that had just occurred between Tim and I.

Thirteen

The Last Time We Were Little Gir

We didn't always have a home. Not a proper one, not with four consistent walls and a roof that stayed predictably put. There was a stretch of time—a chaotic, bewildering blur of Los Angeles freeways and unfamiliar side streets, somewhere between the initial flight from Memphis and the start of our life in Inglewood—where the interior of our car was the only address we possessed. For about a month, the world became our bedroom. The vast, indifferent sky, our ceiling. The asphalt, our constant, rumbling companion. Our address was simply defined by wherever we managed to park that night.

I didn't know the formal, heavy, cold word homelessness then. The concept meant nothing to my young ears. I only knew, with visceral certainty, that we weren't going back to that dirty, temporary house my mom had rented from strangers—a house that smelled of stale, trapped smoke and something damp and profoundly forgotten, a lingering sickness in the air. My mom, the absolute perfectionist, sharp and clean, was fundamentally offended by its unfixable nastiness. It violated her very soul. It was a place she couldn't impose her structural order upon, so she did the only thing she could: she packed us up, and we simply went. We slept in the car, sometimes parked in quiet, dark spots that felt like illicit secrets, the rhythmic hum of the engine serving as a fragile, mechanical lullaby. Sometimes, as a rare, grand treat, we'd sleep in a hotel room, the crisp, clean sheets and tiny, perfect soaps feeling like a transcendent luxury, a brief, blessed escape into a different, stable kind of life. And somehow, through my child's lens, it never felt like a tragedy. It felt, profoundly, like an adventure. A secret, thrilling journey known only to us, a story so bizarre it must be true.

The car itself evolved into a character, a small, battered metal cocoon that held the three of us against the enormity of the rootless world. At night, the seats were hard, unforgiving, but we'd pile every blanket and piece of clothing we possessed to construct soft, warm nests. The windows would fog up immediately with our breath, turning the outside world into blurry, abstract shapes, like a painting made of vapor. In the mornings, the relentless California sun would bake the metal, making the air inside thick and hot, smelling faintly of old french fries and vinyl. We'd roll down the windows, allowing the rushing wind to clean out the air, welcoming the sounds of the city—distant sirens, the rumble of trucks, the quiet chirp of crickets—as our lullabies and alarm clocks. It was a strange, raw kind of freedom, this rootless existence, but it was fiercely, unequivocally ours.

The Cruel, Hilarious Trick

My mom, with her relentless, structural resourcefulness, soon found a Pinto in the classifieds. Back then, people still read actual newspapers, their fingers smudged with ink, meticulously searching for the chance at a fresh start. We took the bus way out to Encino—a long, sprawling, rumbling journey—just to buy it. The sun beat hot on our faces as we waited for Mama to finish the tense, necessary negotiations. When we finally drove it back, that little Pinto's engine purred, its wheels rolled forward, offering a tangible promise of movement, of getting somewhere concrete. It worked. Just fine.

But the very next day, the world decided to play a joke. A cruel, glorious, hilarious trick.

The mechanic informed her: the only gear that functioned was reverse.

Just reverse.

So we drove around Los Angeles in reverse. For a whole, absurd month. It sounds impossible, like a scene ripped straight from a cartoon, yet it was our absolute reality. Every single day. We backed slowly down the street to school, the engine whining a high-pitched protest, waving wildly at confused neighbors who stared with slack-jawed eyes. We navigated crowded parking lots with a strange, careful, backward dance, spinning and turning. Always, always in reverse. The entire world was rushing past us in the rearview mirror, a constant, dizzying rewind. Mama, our fierce, tiny pilot, would lean over the back of the seat, her neck craned, one hand controlling the wheel, the other waving wildly, absolutely laughing.

It was hilarious. Truly, deeply, soul-cleansingly hilarious. Me, Lisa, and my mom were crammed in that small car, seatbelts largely optional, our bodies shaking with suppressed giggles that erupted into outright, uncontrollable belly laughs. We were laughing so hard I genuinely thought we'd float right out the windows, carried away on a wave of pure, unadulterated joy. Our faces were red, our eyes streaming with tears of mirth. That moment, that entire month, had to be before Tim. Before the shadows deepened. Before the laughter in our home became strained, calculated, and rare. The energy was too light, too free, too unburdened by the specific weight of the traumas to come.

My mom was wholly herself—vibrant, engaged, even silly, her usual precision dissolving into helpless, head-thrown-back laughter. And my sister, Lisa, wasn't sulking or spinning in her own private torment. She was just there, profoundly present. Her eyes were bright. She was playing with me, engaging. Like we were both just kids, sharing a secret, absurd joke with the entire world that could not possibly understand our reality.

The Last Time

We played hand games in the car. Our fingers flying, slapping, weaving intricate, complex patterns—a chaotic, beautiful blur of motion in the small space. We sang songs at the top of our lungs, gloriously off-key and joyful, inventing new, ridiculous lyrics as we went. We told silly jokes, the kind that only make sense to two children who share a trauma but have found a temporary escape. I didn't call her names, no sharp words, no cutting remarks. She didn't retaliate, no casual cruelty. She wasn't reckless, wasn't chasing boys or shadows. She was just my big sister, for that brief, shining moment. Her hand in mine, her laughter echoing mine—a pure, untainted bond.

I realized, even then, that she was trying to entertain me. To keep my spirits up. To make the strange, frightening reality of our lives feel less scary. Maybe to distract me from the unspoken worries that surely weighed on Mama. I remember that tiny, quiet voice in my chest saying, Don't make this harder on Mama. That thought, clear as day, was a constant, gentle pressure. I remember thinking, She's going through something massive, something I can't grasp, and I need to be good. I needed to be quiet. To be easy. To not add to her load. I chose to be small. To exist without demanding anything. To be a silent, supportive presence.

I didn't understand the true trauma that haunted my sister, the profound weight my mother carried, or the choices that led us to sleep in a car. But I understood enough to be quiet. To be a good girl. To not add to the burden.

And maybe that's why Lisa and I had that bond. Not the fragile, mended thing we broke and stitched together later, scarred by unspoken pain. But the real one. The first one. The one that felt like breath, like sunshine, like pure, uncomplicated love. It was a secret language only we spoke, a shared understanding of laughter in the face of absurdity, of finding joy in the most unlikely places. A connection forged in the strange, backward journey of that Pinto.

It didn't last. It couldn't. Life would inevitably crack us wide open again, shatter the fragile bubble of our temporary adventure. The shadows would deepen. The laughter would fade, replaced by tension and tears. But for that month? For that precious, absurd month?

We were just two girls and our mother, crammed into a tiny Pinto.

Playing hand games.

Singing off-key songs.

Trying, with everything we had, to be light in a world that felt anything but. A world that was

constantly trying to pull us down, to make us heavy. But for a little while, we floated. We soared.

We laughed. And we were truly home, wherever that Pinto took us.

Notes

Fourteen

Eighth Grade Milestones

The final stretch of eighth grade felt less like a continuous calendar and more like a series of monumental, isolated events—a final, fragile bubble of middle school life before the chaos of high school consumed me. It felt like a strange, ephemeral gift, a necessary space where I finally solidified the feeling that I belonged to something beyond my house, beyond its heavy secrets and its quiet, suffocating storms. I carried my routines like armor: still playing in the band, the loud, joyful blare of my saxophone a defiant sound against the ingrained silence; still loving basketball at the Y, finding solace in the controlled rhythm of the court. I was never on an official team, never seeking the full glare of the spotlight, but that didn't matter. The real, internal victory was finding my best friend, Alisha, my true North, and the courage to build a life outside the war zone of my home.

The Power of Presence

Seventh grade had demanded I remain quiet and guarded. It was almost impossible to form real friendships when the unspoken noise of my home was always louder than anything at school, demanding more of my attention than any teacher. It was hard to let anyone in, to expose the shadows that clung to me. But Alisha's home, with its open door and free-flowing air, was a true haven. Her mother, young and cool, made their home a counter-argument to the silence I knew. There, words were said out loud. Questions were welcomed.

Our group wasn't defined by popularity or exclusive cliques. But because we had Alisha's mom—who trusted us and provided a space of non-judgmental freedom—we felt we could do more than most kids.

The culmination of this newfound freedom was our boy-and-girl slumber party. It wasn't a quiet sleepover; it was an authentic eighth-grade house party, a thrilling, innocent venture into the world of new feelings. The air thrummed with loud music, the bass vibrating through the floorboards, a physical representation of the life I craved. The smell of cheap pizza and sugary soda hung in the air, creating a sensory memory of pure, unadulterated youth. We played games, danced awkwardly, and engaged in playful teasing that felt innocent and thrilling all at once. The lights were low, manufacturing a sense of daring freedom that belied our true ages.

I realized then how much I was still just a girl, navigating new feelings. I was discovering my body's own power: the strange, powerful waves of feeling that would wash over me, leaving me tingling—orgasms I didn't yet have the language to name. In the dark when I was alone, I would touch my body until the explosive moment happened. I had learned that through all the abuse that happened in my family, I never told anyone; I didn't know how or what to say. It was another secret, a private discovery in a life governed by public scrutiny. That strange, strong release just added to my sense of forging my own path, taking care of my own needs. I was becoming fiercely independent. Do I think my story is different than any other teenager discovering themselves? Maybe, maybe not, but this part taught me to hide this portion. I knew nothing about my body, what was happening, my ignorance created a vulnerability, which I am just thankful that nothing worse ever happened to me. That experience added to my desire to share and talk and to never leave people alone with their thoughts or fears.

I was like a fish trying on legs for the first time, exploring new worlds and new things, discovering myself, who I was. I possessed a presence. A way of being, of moving, of laughing, and of holding myself that commanded attention. I was learning to use this power. I didn't want anyone to use me, not like Tim, but I was learning to flirt—nothing aggressive, nothing overtly sexual, just playful. It was a small, thrilling victory: noticing that I could be noticed, and that, when done on my terms, it felt profoundly good. I had started sewing my own clothes, turning the skill Mama taught me into a deliberate act of creation. I was building an external look, a personality, a way to show the world the self I was becoming, even if I wasn't quite sure who she was yet. I was starting to see the value in my own hands, my own talents—a man at Six Flags even offered me a massive order of hats, a genuine business opportunity I was too young to seize, but which affirmed my potential.

The Betrayal

J-ron was a constant, quiet presence in this new world. Until one day at my house, when the usual, simple rules of our friendship shattered entirely. I wasn't supposed to have company—usually it was just Alisha—but this time J-ron was there too. The house, always heavy with the unspoken past, felt smaller, more dangerous, the second he got aggressive. The air in the room thickened, charged with immediate, familiar dread. I remember trying to use my humor, trying to laugh it off, to make the moment disappear like so many other uncomfortable experiences.

But the danger was real. I was scared. Truly scared. A cold knot seized my stomach. I believe, to this day, that if I hadn't been as physically strong as I was—the strength forged in the shadows of my home—and if Alisha hadn't been there, he might have forced himself on us. He tried to take our clothes off. His hands were grabbing, pulling. We fought him off with raw, desperate instinct—pushing, kicking, our bodies a desperate tangle of resistance. Our voices, raw and sharp, shouted the single, necessary word: No.

When he finally left, the silence that followed was crushing, heavy, suffocating. I didn't need any explanation. My internal conclusion was instantaneous: This is why Mama said no company. This is why the doors were always locked. This is why the outside world, even friends, could sometimes be dangerous. The sharp, painful lesson was etched onto my soul. We didn't repeat that mistake.

That assault solidified my desire to create spaces of absolute safety. It is part of why I want a retreat center now. I remember the profound relief of going to the local rec center after school, a genuine safe haven. We played basketball and chess, engaging in simple, pure fun around men who didn't try to touch us. They just played. They just coached. They just watched. And that meant everything. Safe male energy. A space where girls could be girls, and boys could be boys, without crossing the lines of violation. That is the space I want to build again for other girls.

The Door Kicked In

Then came the last, heaviest memory of eighth grade—a memory that still feels like a cold hand pressed directly on my heart.

I came home one day, and our front door was kicked in. Not just a little. Busted open. Splinters of wood were scattered across the porch, a chaotic, shocking mess where the entrance to our home used to be. There was no message from my mom. No note. No explanation. I saw the door hanging crooked, a gaping, ugly hole where safety used to be. The terrifying thing is, I wasn't scared. And I still wonder why. Why didn't fear grip me? I had become so numb, so accustomed to chaos that the sight of a violently breached home registered simply as a normal Tuesday afternoon. I walked upstairs to my mom's room, the floorboards creaking under my feet, and I waited. I waited for her. I waited for an explanation.

Later, my Aunt Lina, her voice soft with overwhelming sorrow, told me the truth. My mom had tried to kill herself. She'd taken pills, a final, desperate attempt to silence the internal pain that had consumed her for years. But there was a tiny, miraculous flicker of hope: she called 911 after, a last, necessary cry for help. She would be gone for a few days, recovering in the hospital. Aunt Lina offered for me to stay with her, to leave the emptiness of the broken house behind. I refused. My voice was firm. I was a big girl. I could handle it.

My sister had run away to Memphis, seeking her own familiar escape. Tim didn't come home either, his absence a sudden, eerie relief. So, I stayed alone. For two full weeks. In that house with the broken door. The silence was deafening. The emptiness vast. I ate cereal. Watched TV. And I waited.

It's funny—I don't even remember the door getting fixed. I just remember her being back. Like nothing happened. Like the two weeks of her absence, the suicide attempt, the gaping hole in our front door, were just a shared nightmare we implicitly agreed to forget. Later I learned she had gone to rehab, but she checked herself out after two weeks because she claimed she was "fine." It was a quick fix, a surface solution that only reinforced the family pattern of denial.

We never talked about what happened. Not the party. Not J-ron. Not the suicide attempt. We laughed. We played. We went right back to the surface, skimming over the deep, dark waters of our lives. My mother was fueled by good vibes and desperate hope, a fragile optimism designed to keep reality at bay. Whenever I tried to talk about anything real, she'd pull me close like a little child and just want to play. To distract. To avoid. To pretend.

By ninth grade, I had made my final, self-defining decision. I was done with public school. Done with the blending. I chose a private school: Serra Catholic School. A new uniform. New rules. A different kind of order. I told my mom I wanted to go. She said yes, hands-off and trusting me to carve out my own future. And just like that, I was enrolled. I wasn't an amazing student there at first, but I was searching. Searching for something different. Searching for the true self, I kept hidden.

Serra brought God back into my life daily, but in the stiff Catholic environment, I felt a sense of silence that brought back fears and didn't allow me to feel safe. In the quiet halls of that private school, where I was starting to choose for myself. To carve out my own path. To finally turn on my own light.

Fifteen

The Cost of Light

I had pushed for the transfer to private school, seeing it not merely as an academic decision but as an act of absolute self-preservation. I thought high school would be different, and in some ways, it was profoundly so. It felt like tearing away one chaotic, dirty chapter to begin a cleaner, quieter one. I had successfully convinced Mama to let me enroll at Serra Catholic School in Gardena, a place that felt like an entire world away from the emotional and physical danger of our Hawthorne home. I wanted something better. Something cleaner. Something quieter. The school had operated as an all-boys institution for sixty years, its long, patriarchal history etched deeply into its brick walls. We were the first girls—a small, highly visible group of ninth-graders walking into a world full of tenth, eleventh, and twelfth-grade boys. You can imagine the immediate, visceral effect: the constant, heavy scrutiny, the whispers that followed us like exhaust smoke, the sudden, paralyzing awkward silences when we entered a room, and the nervous, uncomfortable laughter. It was a strange, charged, and utterly new landscape I had to navigate.

The Sanctuary of the Male Friend

In this unexpected environment, I found friends, but what I found in the male friendships was a complete surprise and a different, profoundly needed form of safety. These boys were not the predators I had learned to defend against; they were a refuge from the constant, predatory gaze I had known elsewhere. They stood up for me, their voices loud and clear in the hallways, acting as an implicit, physical shield. They talked to me—truly talked—about homework, their dreams, and the gloriously silly, unimportant things that consume teenagers. They made me feel like I belonged, like I was an accepted, unthreatening part of their world. With my quiet strength and my developing body, I was instinctively relegated to the role of the little sister. I was not the girl they tried to pursue; I was not the object of their desire or violation. I was simply one of them.

And I didn't just like that role. I craved it. I clung to it with the ferocity of someone drowning who finds a solid branch. This platonic closeness was a healing balm I didn't know existed. We built a small, protective ecosystem together. I would analyze their social dynamics, offer blunt assessments of their crushes, and translate the confusing emotional signals of the girls they pursued. They, in turn, offered me a reliable covering, their presence implicitly communicating to the wider world that I was protected and off-limits. I learned that safety wasn't always a locked door; sometimes, it was a visible community of allies.

Now, looking back with the chilling clarity of hindsight, I saw their world. I saw those same boys engage in the casual hookups, the whisper campaigns, the broken hearts, and the inevitable, quiet shame that spread through the school like wildfire. Yet, they never once tried that with me. The boundary was absolute. I still don't know the singular reason why. Perhaps they sensed the quiet, non-negotiable boundary I held, the shield of innocence—a protection that was both intentional and unconsciously radiating from the girl who had survived too much. Or perhaps, and this is the hope I prefer to hold, God simply protected me, assigning a silent guardian angel to watch over the most vulnerable part of my adolescence. Either way, I found a profound, essential safety in their constant presence, a sanctuary.

I am still uncertain if the need was entirely mine—the need to be treated like a little sister to feel that pure, uncomplicated, platonic love—or if they needed it too, a relief from the performance of toxic masculinity. The dynamic worked perfectly. For me, it was the first true glimpse of light and safety I had ever known from the masculine world. I could share the turbulence inside me—the fear, the confusion, the lingering shadows of the chaos at home—without the paralyzing fear of judgment or violation. For them, I believe I offered something equally rare: a female friend who could speak honestly about what girls felt, without pretense or social game-playing. I was direct. I was honest. Together, in that small, unlikely circle, we enacted a quiet revolution. It was my first real experience of mutual light with males—a balanced, reciprocal connection. This vulnerability, met with understanding rather than violation, built something fundamentally new inside me. I began to trust my voice in their presence, allowing glimpses of the woman I was determined to become.

The Fear of the Spotlight

That year was also marked by tentative, external explorations of attraction. I had three boyfriends—Jason, Liam, and briefly Aaron. They were fleeting, tentative connections, more experiments in communication than deep relationships. We were all figuring out the vast, awkward landscape of romance. The encounters were safe and kind; they didn't push, they didn't demand. Simultaneously, I was starting to notice my physical self—not just the functional strength of my athleticism, but my curves, my shape. I was becoming aware of how the world looked at me—the way eyes lingered, the way conversations shifted—and how I wanted to be looked at. I wasn't trying to be flirty; I just wanted to be seen without being consumed. To feel visible and still safe. To be known without being violated.

The man who truly validated my internal architecture was Coach H. His name, perhaps a strange irony, belonged to the man who would give me a critical piece of my identity. He was the first man who truly talked to me as an individual. Not about boys or grades, but about me. He saw me. He truly saw the athlete in me, recognizing the raw strength I had only ever used for defense against the world. I played basketball for him, the predictable squeak of the court a familiar comfort. He also challenged me to join the cross country team, an impossible concept for a girl who had never run a sustained mile in her life. But I tried. I pushed myself to the absolute edge of my physical endurance. And it paid off. When over a hundred girls tried out for basketball, I made the team. I made the starting five.

For the first time in my life, I felt seen not for my ability to hide, but for my raw, undeniable talent. My effort. My potential.

And that terrified me.

I had spent my entire life being the strong one, the clever one, the one who could handle anything in the shadows. But now, I was being held up to the public light for something that mattered deeply to my core self. My body, which was my fortress, suddenly betrayed me. Every time Coach H put me in the game, under the harsh, bright lights of the gymnasium, I froze. My muscles locked into a terrifying rigidity. My mind went blank. I choked. The physical sensations were overwhelming—the heat of the lights, the roar of the crowd, the specific, terrifying pressure of expectation. The basketball felt heavy and foreign in my hands. The hoop seemed miles away, unreachable. I would cry, silent, burning tears that blurred my vision. My lungs would seize, my breath shallow. It felt like failure, but it was deeper. It was as if the emotional weight of my buried fears, the unseen traumas, had finally seized control, shutting my body down in public. I had perfected the art of invisibility for so long that I simply did not know how to exist, powerfully, in the spotlight. The spotlight felt like a burning interrogation.

Coach H, his face etched with concern, would look down the bench and ask, "You ready?" And all I could offer was a silent shake of the head or a frantic, fake adjustment to my shoelaces, desperate to avoid his gaze, desperate to avoid the expectation. In practice, I was brilliant. I excelled. But in the game, when the pressure was on, when eyes were watching? I disappeared.

My talent simply vanished.

The Cost of Light and the Art of Sacrifice

This was the cost of light.

To be seen was to risk everything I had worked to protect. It wasn't merely the risk of failure on the court; it was the risk of exposure. The risk of vulnerability. The terrifying, raw shame of being truly known by others. I didn't have the words for it then, but I know now: my body wasn't scared of the game. It was profoundly scared of the spotlight. It was terrified of what being seen might bring—the scrutiny, the potential for harm, the demand to perform the perfection I knew was a lie.

At home, the tension lingered, the silence persisted. But something essential was shifting inside me. I was writing more, filling my journals faster. This passion, surprisingly, was something my mother and I shared. She was a writer, too, an "advisor-writer," her own words filling pages. She always encouraged my writing, asking to read it, praising the raw honesty she found there.

The only place my mother let life be raw was on paper. In the real, public world, there was no space for talking about things. The abuse. Her own haunting past. Why she drank. The deep, festering wounds of our family history. It all stayed rigorously hidden behind polished surfaces and forced smiles. But on paper, the boundary shifted—it was safe. There, in the private world of words, we could hint at the truths. My stories became my life, my explicit lifeline.

As I sit here now, decades later, I wonder if that encouragement was her final, desperate instruction: "This is how I survived. This is how you can too." Her faith in my pen was her final act of provision.

The family narrative always focused on how Mama left her career—her dreams of being an actress, a singer, a star—to raise us. But maybe she left that world not just for us, but because of what it demanded of her. The profound darkness it required. She had been almost raped several times, she hinted, told she had to exchange favors for roles, for a chance at the spotlight. The darkness was a price she refused to pay. She knew the spotlight demanded a secret shame, a moral concession she would not make, choosing silence and order over that specific form of degradation. She chose to be a fixer of houses, not a star, because that path allowed her to retain control over her own body and dignity. This act of sacrifice—the rejection of her greatest dream to escape the predatory demands of the male gaze—was the most powerful lesson she taught me.

Maybe she gave me the light by encouraging my writing because she knew she couldn't give it to Lisa—Lisa's light was already taken, ripped away by a monster. But for me? She offered a different path.

But real light came at a price I was only just beginning to comprehend: The price of being seen. The price of vulnerability. The price of stepping out from the shadows I had built for survival. And I was now, finally, ready to begin paying that cost.

Sixteen

The Unspoken Truth

The decision to leave the relative quiet of Serra Catholic and transfer to Leuzinger High in my sophomore year was a conscious, almost defiant plunge back into the raw, unvarnished energy of South Central LA. The best, most essential part of that move was simple, immediate, and profound: I got to be with Alisha again. My best friend. My anchor. Her unfiltered laughter was a familiar, necessary melody cutting through the new, pervasive chaos. I didn't know it then, but Leuzinger, with its wild, unvarnished truth and its relentless pace, would ultimately be the place that helped me find my true voice—not just the loud, defiant one I used for defense, but the deeper, truer one that spoke my truth without flinching and demanded the world listen.

This school was not an institution; it was a force of nature. A living, breathing testament to the fierce, raw, often desperate energy of the city. It had been through everything—gang tensions, riots, lockdowns—the constant, high-frequency hum of survival pervading the air of every classroom and hallway. Yet, it was also a place of vibrant, defiant beauty, a powerful tapestry of faces and cultures. People flowed in from every corner of the world, from the islands to different continents. Different languages mingled and clashed in the hallways, creating a chaotic kind of freedom, a beautiful, messy blend I instantly recognized as authentic. We didn't learn much from the textbooks in the conventional, rigid way they taught in private schools.

But we learned something infinitely more valuable: how to see each other. We learned how to survive together. How to find a common, necessary ground in the shared struggle of being young and under siege **in a complicated world. The lack of pretension was a comfort I desperately needed.**

The Cuban Bridge

In the ninth grade, amidst the mounting pressure of school and the shadows at home, I found weightlifting. It was an unexpected, powerful kind of escape, a new, physical way to impose order and feel strong when my emotional world was pure anarchy. I was only 5'5" and 120 pounds, yet I could bench press 145 pounds. The iron in my hands felt cold, heavy, and brutally honest, but the moment I pushed it up, it felt light, obedient solely to my will. I could squat 180 and leg press 500. Each lift was a therapeutic release. Each rep was a surge of undeniable, self-generated power. That was the first time I truly understood that my relentless relationship with health and strength was not vanity; it was a profound survival tactic. It was my physical therapy. It was my quiet, solitary rebellion against the relentless feeling of powerlessness that governed my life outside the gym. The gruff, kind football coach even used me to shame the boys, making me lift heavier weights than they could, a perverse public validation of the strength I was determined to possess. My muscles became a dense, visible argument against the emotional fragility I had to hide.

I allowed a soft, kind boyfriend named Anthony, a Cuban boy, into my carefully constructed life. He didn't speak much English, and I didn't speak much Spanish. This linguistic gap forced a profound, early intimacy: we wrote letters, our hesitant, careful words serving as a tender bridge between cultures and silences. We sought out quiet, non-threatening places just to be together. His eyes were kind and gentle. His touch was light and respectful. He was a soft comfort in a world that often felt harsh, an intentional space of peace I allowed into my life.

The Internal Fire and the External Riot

While I built this quiet, controlled world, the city's inherent rage reached its boiling point. Near the end of tenth grade, the external world mirrored the internal chaos I was desperate to suppress. The city erupted. The LA Riots were consuming neighborhoods, the smoke a thick, dark cloud on the horizon, a constant, physical reminder of the rage simmering just beneath the surface of all our lives. And something internal caught fire too. A quiet, necessary blaze ignited within me, fueled by fear and intellectual curiosity.

I was devouring everything I could get my hands on: Dr. King, his words a call for peace and justice; Malcolm X, his fierce, unyielding truth a terrifying but vital validation of my own anger; Gandhi, his quiet power proving that transformation was an internal, deliberate process. I was desperately trying to intellectually process the world falling apart around me, trying to find meaning in the overwhelming chaos. I filled journals with frantic energy, writing about the city burning, about the disintegration of the public world, and about my fierce, quiet attempts to hold myself together inside it. The words on the page were my only consistent anchor against the rising tide of existential fear.

The Humiliation and the Breakthrough

In English class, a young white teacher, her eyes bright with passion and naive hope, invited me to join a theater tour. "We perform speeches," she said, her voice earnest, "and speak truth around LA. To schools, to community centers. To people who need to hear it." I said yes. A quiet, determined, profoundly fearful yes. I thought it was the final, necessary battle: a way to finally conquer the fear that still lingered, the deep-seated terror of being seen and heard. I believed this stage was the ultimate forge for my voice.

But the first time I stepped onto that stage—the unforgiving lights hot, the faces of the audience a terrifying blur in the darkness—the paralyzing freeze response, the same one that seized me when Tim violated me, took immediate control of my body. My muscles locked. My mind went blank. I peed. For real. A warm, humiliating, uncontrollable trickle down my leg. The raw, absolute fear of public exposure returned, a cold, total, paralyzing grip. My stomach clenched. My breath caught, seized by the sheer terror of having my physical, vulnerable self exposed.

The familiar voice of the trauma demanded I retreat: Be still. Be silent. You are exposed. You are humiliated. Disappear.

But this time, fueled by the memory of the closet and the vow I had made to the pen, I did not run. I fought through the shame. I pushed past the heat of the humiliation. I delivered the speech. My voice, which started trembling with fear, grew stronger with every word, fueled by the sheer desperation of defiance. That terrifying moment on stage—that visceral, absolute loss of control in front of strangers—became the moment I was never silenced again. The words, once trapped inside the closet and the journals, were finally, irrevocably free. I learned that the fear of the spotlight was a manageable pain; it was secondary to the shame of staying quiet and letting the trauma win.

The Finality of the Choice

The chaos soon forced my hand again, demanding a permanent choice. The culmination of the riots locked us inside the school. The air outside was thick with sirens and shouts. They had put up massive, 12- to 15-foot fences around the school—tall metal cages—to keep us in and the escalating violence out. When the shattering glass and angry shouts reached us, we were trapped. Like caged animals. I hid in the theater with my troupe leader, behind the heavy velvet curtain, the darkness a strange, familiar comfort that reminded me of the closet. I remember thinking, my mind absolutely clear despite the palpable fear: I will never come back here again. Not to this school. Not to this kind of fear.

When I finally got home, the air still thick with the smell of smoke and existential fear, I delivered my ultimatum to Mama: "Find me a private school or I'm dropping out." My voice was firm, unyielding, a weapon I had finally learned to use for practical self-defense. She looked at me, her eyes tired, but she didn't argue. That summer, I found South Bay Lutheran. A tiny school—109 students total. A small, quiet haven.

That same summer, the one after the riots, I had my final, devastating lesson in the cost of light. I ran into Aubrey at the arcade. After a confrontation I initiated—demanding he acknowledge his rudeness—sparks flew. He became my first great love. He saw past the mask. I made the conscious decision to give him my body in our senior year. It was my decision, an act of autonomy I cherished. We were great. Until I got accepted to college and realized it was puppy love—a sweet, innocent thing, but not built to withstand the distance.

The Thirty-Year Silence

But the true price was exacted later. Freshman year, a long letter arrived from Alisha. It told a story that shattered my world: she had something to tell me about her and Aubrey. At the time, I wasn't really worried. When I returned to LA, I sat on a white couch with Alisha, her mom, and two new friends telling me of all the things Aubrey had done to try to have a relationship with her, that it had gone on for months. I am not sure where, but my brain turned off, all I could think was how could they hide this from me, they were a safe space in a world where I desperately needed a safe space. I felt betrayal and hurt like nothing I had ever felt before. It wasn't about Aubrey; he was a boy, sure, my first love, but a teenage boy nonetheless. They were my safe space. Why didn't she tell me? My mind thought there must be more that she is not telling me, a silent feeling on our friendship that lasted 30 plus years, I would always believe that there was more to the story. It wasn't until I was writing this book that I decided to break that silence to hear her story.

I was mad not about the boy, but because they—Alisha, her mother, her friends—had seen me, knew me, loved me, and still collectively lied. I felt like it was a lie of omission. The cost of light, again. The price of being seen and then betrayed.

It would take me thirty more years to learn the full, heartbreaking truth. Alisha never actually slept with Aubrey. Her letter, fueled by fear and bad advice, was trying to tell me about his unwanted advances and her rejections, but her circle convinced her I would never believe her over the popular boy. The distance fueled my imagination, twisting the silence into confirmation of my worst fears. Alisha and I were burdened with our own traumas, and our raw, true friendship couldn't provide what we needed when our first true rift occurred. We didn't know how to fight for the friendship we found, and it was lost for decades. I wish her nothing but love and peace, and I will always be grateful for the friendship we had at such a tumultuous time.

But our story has a final grace: We did talk. I hate that it took thirty years to have that conversation, to finally turn on the light in that dark, misunderstood corner of our past. We were both victims of a different kind of silence, a different kind of harm. She was a young woman who felt harassed, and I felt like a secret world was lived in a place I felt safe.

I got accepted to Chico State—my top choice. I chose it because it was the farthest place from my house, a thousand miles away. It wasn't running from fear; it was running toward my own future.

That day I left for college, I knew LA had nothing left for me. No more safe places. No more illusions. I was ready to write. To get my degree. To set the world on fire with my truth.

Seventeen

The Discovery of Loss

The chaos of my adolescence was suddenly, unexpectedly punctuated by a love so profound and so simple it felt like a deliberate act of grace: Aubrey. After the dramatic and exhausting circumstances surrounding our initial meeting—the sharp confrontation in the arcade, the deliberate audacity of my demanding his name—who could have predicted that we would evolve into true, necessary safe spaces for one another? Aubrey was, on the surface, a handsome, cocky boy on the verge of becoming a professional baseball player. Yet, like me and so many others who walked the strained hallways of our high school, he was at his core just a lost little boy searching for ground. On the outside, he presented a flawless show face, a rigid mask of cocky male confidence, but beneath it beat a heart, I knew, of genuine gold.

We fell into love quickly, the emotional stakes rising with a speed that mirrored the suddenness of my childhood flight from Memphis. But more than anything, we were profoundly, urgently friends. This bond became a mirror reflecting my deepest needs: I was a girl whose entire emotional currency was based on the premise of self-sufficiency, a girl who desperately needed to feel consistently safe around a male.

That acute need for safety gave Aubrey something essential to hold onto. It gave him something profound to look forward to, something noble to esteem himself to be. He wasn't just a boyfriend; he was my chosen protector, my chosen guard against the shadows. He tried with a relentless, sincere effort to ensure that I felt safe, consistently showing up for me in ways I had only ever read about in books. This quiet, non-sexual duty to protect defined our intimacy and provided the framework for our connection, giving meaning to his strong, but ultimately wandering, eye.

Heartbreak

The strength of my identity was built on an expert ability to avoid feeling and expressing want or need. It was a lesson brutally etched onto my soul when my father casually said no to my request to stay the night after his fleeting visit. I was the master of detachment.

Then came the mistake. In the very beginning of our tentative relationship, acting on the strong, independent little girl I fiercely proclaimed myself to be—the girl who believed she was immune to the rules of fragile attachment—I went out and kissed another boy, Kevin. I believed, with a cold, terrifying certainty, that I was emotionally immune to consequences. Somehow, Aubrey found out. His reaction was a terrifying mixture of pain and possessiveness. He was determined to make my life miserable, but in the same breath, he made it agonizingly clear that he didn't want to let me go. He called to break up with me, and in the calculating, protective machinery of my mind, I thought: It will be fine. I am prepared for this.

But I was shattered. I was devastated.

I cried. Not the quiet, dignified, contained tears I had learned to shed in the isolation of my pillow. I cried uncontrollably. I had never cried over something so purely emotional before. Never. Not even the loss of my father—that loss was categorized as a systemic failure, a quiet disappointment that required logical compensation. But this was raw, searing, unexpected loss. It was a shocking, terrifying new feeling. I had never allowed myself to want something—a person, a connection, a shared future—let alone express the feelings of need and devastation that followed its loss.

Why the hell was I crying uncontrollably? The tears, the sheer, physical anguish, were a profound betrayal of the fortress I had spent years constructing. I think the sheer force of my unraveling shocked him, too, because as I sat there, sobbing into the phone, I realized he was crying as well. We were two young people, sixteen and seventeen years old, exposed and vulnerable, suddenly faced with the truth that we were genuinely, deeply in love.

The Family I Never Had

We chose to move forward, attempting to act as if the betrayal had been smoothed over by the sheer force of our mutual need. But I believe he remained subtly hurt, his confidence fractured, which explained the strong, wandering eye he continued to possess throughout our relationship. We dated for two years. He was my first love in all ways, a profound physical and emotional experience that I chose. He was the first male I willingly gave myself to, an act of autonomy I cherished. I chose him because he had proven, even in his flawed way, that he could be a safe place.

Our relationship was not simply defined by the sexual and romantic discovery; it was sustained by the simple, enduring fact that we were, above all else, friends. He was a boy with a strong, predictable ego and a sometimes wandering eye, yet I was a girl whose foundational need for male safety gave him the necessary purpose to anchor himself. He tried relentlessly hard to make sure I felt safe, consistently showing up for me and seeing my complex life with love, even when he was just a young, cocky male trying to figure out the contours of his own existence.

The true grace of Aubrey's life was his family. They were a massive, welcoming, embracing unit—the large, loud, predictable family unit I had always craved and never possessed. They loved me immediately and unconditionally, pulling me into the fold of their stable chaos. Their kindness, their acceptance, and the sheer presence of their familial unit were a profound and necessary healing balm against the cold silence and isolation of my own home. I loved them deeply, and they will always hold a special, foundational place in my heart for providing that glimpse of belonging.

The True Rift and the Legacy of the Pen

We broke up after senior year. The distance of college provided the clean, necessary cut, ending what was, in retrospect, a sweet, innocent, but fundamentally unsustainable puppy love. Yet, even that separation was a profound grief, a second loss that marked the growth I had achieved.

Aubrey will always hold a special place in my heart for the thousands of long, shared phone calls, the quiet walks in the parks, and the simple, monumental act of seeing my life and still choosing to love me.

The ultimate tragedy of this chapter is that when the true test came—the rift with Alisha over the thirty-year lie—the vulnerability that Aubrey had taught me to embrace led to profound misunderstanding and loss. Alisha and I were both burdened by our individual traumas, and while our friendship was raw and true, it was fundamentally incapable of surviving that first true emotional rift. We lost what was once the most important external stability in my life, and I never truly knew why for three decades.

The pain of the friendship loss, and the loss of Aubrey, was so absolute because they were the only two places I allowed my expert avoidance to fail. I allowed myself to want them, and when I lost them, I learned that the emotional devastation of true loss was more shattering than the cold, predictable logic of familial chaos. I finally understood why my mother retreated into perfectionism and silence: the pain of feeling is a terrifying, consuming fire.

I wish both Aubrey and Alisha nothing but love and peace, and will always be grateful for the friendship and the lessons we shared at such a tumultuous time in my life. I don't think either of us recognized what we truly were for each other—a lifeline, a map, a mirror—nor did we know how to fight for the complex, fragile friendship we found. Maybe one day, decades after the run, we will.

Eighteen

My Angel

The surface of my life during my senior year looked impeccably finished, polished smooth like the floors of my mother's perfect houses. It was a fresh coat of paint applied over old, deep cracks. I was back in private school, the quiet, predictable halls of South Bay Lutheran offering a stark, welcome contrast to the wild, consuming energy of Leuzinger. I even had a boyfriend, a comfortable, steady presence who provided a predictable rhythm. My focus was absolute: grounded, centered, with my sights locked onto college, locked onto the promise of permanent escape. I was playing basketball again—a starter, my name called out before the game, a profound, public thrill that still surprised and humbled me.

I hadn't completely eliminated my fear; it still lingered, a deep, cold dread that would rise instantly when someone came aggressively into my face to guard me, their breath hot on my skin, their body too close. The old, familiar terrors still threatened my control. But I showed up. I pushed through the panic. I was actively testing my sea legs in the light, learning, painstakingly, to swim in the vast open, even when the waves felt overwhelming. My coaches—white men this time, offering a stability different from the coaches who had seen me fly before—were kind. They were present. They believed in me with a quiet, unwavering faith, their confidence a steady, necessary hand on my back. This small school offered something I hadn't felt in a long time: absolute safety and structure. A predictable rhythm that made my internal world feel less like anarchy.

But shadows don't care about the surface. They cling. They burrow. They wait for the moment of deepest vulnerability to reveal their enduring power.

My sister, Lisa, had moved back from Memphis, arriving like a ghost from a past I was determined to outrun. And she brought my nephew with her. He was only two, a tiny, bright spark of life, a physical miracle of pure, untainted innocence. I loved him instantly, deeply, fiercely, with an intensity that shocked and surprised my emotionally fortified heart. But the love I had for him was not just sweet or simple—it was born out of a moment of internal confrontation that still makes me shudder, a cold, total tremor running through my body even now. It was a moment that solidified a terrifying truth I had only glimpsed before.

The Internal Demon and the Visceral Recoil

That summer, when she first had him, I had gone to Memphis to be with her. The air was thick and humid, heavy with the weight of unspoken things. I was babysitting him one afternoon, just me and this tiny little boy who couldn't even speak, who offered no resistance, who possessed no shield. His eyes, wide, deep, and trusting, looked up at me—eyes of absolute innocence and purity.

And that's when the thought hit me. It was sharp, wrong, and terrifyingly clear. A raw whisper originating from the dark place I thought I had sealed off years ago. It was a voice that sounded exactly like the vampire.

The absolute sickness that flooded my body in that precise moment—the sudden, visceral wave of nausea, the cold, clammy sweat that broke out over my skin—is something I will never, ever forget. It was an involuntary, physical recoil. Physically, my stomach violently flipped, my muscles seized and tensed. Spiritually, my soul recoiled with a terror far deeper than physical pain, shrinking violently from the darkness that dared to claim me. I wanted to throw up, to physically purge the vile thought from my mind, to reject the legacy of the trauma that demanded perpetuation.

I remember seizing him, this small, innocent boy, my angel, and holding him tighter than I had ever held anything. I was holding him not out of danger from him, but out of a sudden, overwhelming, terrifying understanding of what it meant to consciously choose love. To consciously choose light. To actively choose to protect instead of perpetuate the inherited chain of pain.

That was the absolute first time in my life I knew what love truly was. Not just as a fleeting emotion or a warm feeling. But as a fundamental, fierce, unwavering decision. A conscious, absolute act of will that required more strength than all the muscles I had ever forged in the weight room. I chose to protect him. I chose to break the cycle. I chose to be different. I knew then, with a profound certainty that shook my entire being, that life is not about chance; it is all about choices. And that my job, my singular purpose, was to make choices that did no harm to myself and, more importantly, did no harm to others. I had known this truth intellectually, in the quiet pages of my journal. But loving him, truly loving this tiny, helpless being, made it concrete. It solidified the concept in my mind, etching it permanently into my soul. Loving a thing, truly loving with an open heart, is a gift from God. And he, my nephew, my angel, was that holy gift.

The Confrontation and the New Boundary

This profound, defining moment became my compass. The memory of my nephew's trusting eyes, the lingering sickness in my stomach from the internal battle, fueled my rage when the external threat appeared.

And so, when one of the grown men around my sister—her boyfriend's friend, a hulking, loud presence in the small, chaotic room—came upstairs, took off his shirt, his body too big, too close, and sat beside me with his arm wrapped around me like I was his property, I didn't hesitate. Not for a fraction of a second. The choice was terrifyingly clear.

I went off.

I cursed him from here to Sunday, my voice a raw, unholy sound ripped from the deepest parts of my soul. "Who the hell do you think you are? Aren't you a grown-ass man? Am I not a child? Are you sick?" I tore into him, with all the explosive power of someone who had just faced her own deepest shadow and lived to tell the tale. My words, sharp and precise, cut through the heavy, stale air, not just challenging him, but exposing his vile intent.

My sister and her boyfriend just laughed. A hollow, familiar, dismissive sound that utterly negated my courage. "Told you not to mess with her," they said, as if it were a joke, as if I were merely a wild animal to be warned against, not a young woman asserting her inherent human dignity.

But it wasn't funny. Not to me. Not to the part of me that had just come face to face with the kind of shadow that doesn't leave fingerprints. The kind that leaves invisible, permanent scars. I had already done the sacred work no child should have to do—choosing to protect instead of perpetuate, choosing light over darkness. And here was someone immediately testing that choice, pushing violently at the precious boundaries I had just so fiercely drawn in my soul.

The crushing realization was this: I shouldn't have had to be the one to draw that line. That was the adults' job. That was their profound responsibility. There was pride that I did, yes, but beneath it was a profound, burning anger that no one else stepped up.

That same silence that didn't protect us, that allowed the monsters to roam free, was present again, a heavy, suffocating weight in the air. But I didn't say the final truth then. Not the anger, not the accusation, not the full truth about the shadows that clung to his mother. I didn't want to hurt them. That's how I saw it: I was the youngest in the house, but I felt it was my impossible job to protect. To keep peace. To carry the unspoken burdens for everyone else.

Stolen Light

That summer in Memphis, the internal demon was banished. The vile echo of my own past that whispered, He can't talk. He's helpless. You could do what was done to you, was met with my soul's visceral rejection. My whole body recoiled, my stomach churning. And I knew—deep in my soul—my job in this world was to break the cycle. Never to pass it on. Never to cause harm. Never to become the monster. That was the last time the darkness tried to claim me.

He taught me love. That small, innocent boy. He taught me the fierce, protective kind of love that demands action, that demands a choice, that demands a change of legacy.

From that moment on, I cared for him like he was mine. He was my purpose. He came with me everywhere—basketball away games, his tiny hand in mine as we walked through noisy gyms. School events, sitting quietly in the audience, his eyes wide, trusting. Friends assumed he was my child because my schedule revolved entirely around him—because my sister, love her deeply, wasn't in a place to mother. She slept all day, lost in her own pain. She yelled when he cried, her patience thin, frayed. She didn't know how to care for something because no one had ever truly cared for her. She was a broken girl, trying to navigate a world that had stolen her light.

When I look back now, I see her not as a bad mother, but as a broken girl. A victim of a darkness she couldn't escape. Those six months she spent in that hellhole—they removed something vital from her soul and never gave it back. The vampire didn't just bite her. It killed the part of her that could see light, that could nurture, that could simply be.

And all the while, I was playing sports. I was trying. I was showing up. Basketball was more than a game. It was a physical battleground where I fought desperately to feel free. Every time I froze when someone guarded me too close, their body pressing against mine, the old fears rising, I still kept going. I wasn't healed. But I was moving. I hadn't found my full voice yet. But I was stepping into it, one defiant dribble at a time.

That court was where I could feel my body and believe in it again. Believe in its strength, its power, its ability to move without fear. It was the place I started to remember what strength felt like without the shadow of violation. My coaches saw me. And even when I hesitated, even when my fear showed, they never pulled that belief away. They kept pushing. They kept believing.

This was me, still dancing in the shadow—but beginning to face the light. Beginning to claim my own space. Beginning to heal for the sake of the angel I held in my arms.

Nineteen

The Cop, the Hammer, and the Exi

By the time junior year ended, I had accumulated a war chest of survival skills. I had survived so many hidden battles, so many quiet wars fought relentlessly within the walls of our home, and inside the fragile confines of my own skin. I had constructed the emotional mask, found my voice in the closet, and built my body into a fortress. But nothing, absolutely nothing, can truly prepare you for the moment when the entire scaffolding of your childhood narrative collapses. It is the shattering moment when the hope you've fiercely maintained—the belief that the adults or the system will eventually swoop in and make it right—dies a sudden, violent death. You realize, with chilling finality, that the saviors you waited for are never coming. They are not coming to fix it. They are not coming to say sorry. And they are not coming to truly see you, the real you, hidden behind the mask of compliance.

I came home from school one afternoon, and the physical environment screamed that something seismic had occurred. The air felt profoundly strange. Too quiet. The usual, distant hum of traffic, the routine shouts of neighborhood kids, seemed muted, stifled. Then I saw it: the front door was wide open. Not kicked in, not busted from a fight—just standing open, ajar, like something had finally, irrevocably left and was never coming back. The silence that followed was heavy, expectant. It was a new, terrifying kind of quiet that descended upon the house.

The Irony of Justice

Tim was gone.

But not before my mother was taken away in handcuffs.

He had systematically broken her for years, a slow, grinding cruelty that wore down her once-fierce spirit. He hurt me, through his invasive touches and casual cruelty. He hurt my sister, twisting her already damaged soul. From the start of my second grade through the end of my eleventh, Tim was the perpetual shadow in our home—a pervasive, menacing presence that colored every corner of our lives.

When Mama, pushed past the absolute, final limit of her endurance, finally picked up a hammer and said enough—her voice a raw, desperate cry of self-defense—he called the cops. And they listened. They always, chillingly, listened to him.

That moment should have been a burst of light, a moment of profound, liberating release. Instead, it left a jagged, painful fissure in my entire understanding of justice. The man who had broken us, who had systematically dismantled our peace through emotional and physical violence, was given the stage to claim victimhood. He played the part of the injured party. And the woman who had finally fought back, who had finally dared to defend her family and her sanctuary, was dragged out like she was the monster. Her wrists bound. Her face, a mask of profound, weary defiance.

As I watched the police car pull away, the realization crystallized into a single, terrifying thought: they're still not coming for us. Not for the real victims. Not for the broken girls who stood watching the scene from the doorway.

I was suddenly forced to confront the systemic blindness we had lived under. When my sister was eight, brutally abused and traumatized under the guise of family, no one called the cops. No one intervened. No one brought her home until a vigilant school counselor noticed the tell-tale bruises. Even when she physically returned, she didn't really come home; the vibrant girl I knew was gone, replaced by a shadow. Glimpses of the old Lisa remained, and I tried desperately to hold on, but my own trauma made it impossible to fully reach her. I wasn't a mother. I was a child, struggling to survive my own battles.

There was no CPS. Not for me. Not for our house. No social workers. No official intervention. Only the knowing looks and the long silences of family members who saw too much and said too little. The system, which was ostensibly designed to protect, remained blind to our suffering until it became convenient for our abuser.

The irony was bitter, a harsh taste I will never forget. In the world outside our home, the cops would handcuff us in alleys, their voices sharp, their hands rough, searching our bodies for drugs we didn't have, treating us with immediate suspicion. But inside the house, when Tim called them? They came like clockwork. They were polite. Familiar. Their voices were calm. They saw only the narrative Tim presented. They never saw the fear in our eyes. They never heard the silent screams.

The Final Boundary

When Mama, finally pushed beyond human endurance, fought back, the price was her arrest. That moment, however, was the profound turning point for her. It was a hard, cold realization. She saw Tim not just as a tormentor, but as a manipulative architect of the system. She realized he had to go. For good. The illusion of hope was finally shattered.

And me? I understood the laws. I always did. Even as a teenager, I knew—if you hit someone, you're going to jail. Back then, before they started arresting both parties no matter what, the victim had the power to stop the cycle by refusing to press charges. But Mama never did. Tim did. And that was the essential difference. The man who had terrorized us finally used the system because it served him, and Mama paid the price.

We stayed in a hotel for a while after that, just the two of us, Mama and me. The quiet of the room felt strange. Too empty. Then we moved back to the beige house in Hawthorne. And Tim never came back. His shadow finally lifted.

He tried to return. He called. His voice was a persistent, echoing threat. But this time, Mama was steel. Her resolve was absolute and unwavering. She said no. Her voice, usually soft, was firm, a boundary finally, irrevocably drawn.

We started talking more that year, or at least spending more time together. The air between us felt lighter, less burdened. But we never talked about anything real. Not the arrest. Not the years of abuse. Not the deep, festering wounds. Only laughter and games. Stories that skimmed the surface, light and airy. My mother wasn't built for deep talks—she was fueled by positive energy, by the fierce necessity of maintaining the illusion of normalcy. Whenever I tried to broach something real, she'd pull me close like I was still a little girl and change the subject. She just wanted to laugh, to play. That was her way of surviving. Her way of coping. She wasn't perfect, but she was present. And sometimes, in a house where everything had been so loud and painful, presence in silence was its own kind of gift. A quiet comfort.

Holding the Flashlight

And me? I had survived another ending. Another silence. Another chapter closed.

But I was fundamentally, irrevocably changed. I was done letting silence feel like home. Done letting the chaos define me.

I wasn't waiting for someone to save me anymore. That desperate hope had died on the lawn of our house, replaced by a fierce, internal, unshakeable self-reliance.

I was the one holding the flashlight.

And I was finally, utterly willing to aim it where the darkness used to be. To illuminate the hidden corners of the past. To expose the shadows. To tell the story. This was the moment I claimed the full power of my own narrative.

The exit wound had finally closed, leaving behind a scar of strength.

Twenty

The Mirror

A t seventeen, standing on the precipice of escape and adulthood, the world felt less like a coherent stage and more like a kaleido-scope—a relentless tumble of shifting colors and sharp, unpredictable edges. I started writing poems I never intended for another soul to read, poems that functioned as deep-sea sounding devices for my buried self. I kept them strictly private, not because I was ashamed of the raw truths they unearthed, but because I hadn't yet acquired the vocabulary to explain their existence. I lacked the spoken language, the easy, normalized words necessary to articulate the fire that burned in my belly: a quiet, simmering rage for the injustices witnessed; a vast, echoing silence that was the canyon carved out by years of trauma; a shifting, elusive identity I couldn't quite grasp. And beneath it all, an undeniable, foundational truth: the constant, subtle weight of being a girl in a world that fundamentally expected so little from girls like me.

The Politics of Invisibility

Not just a girl. A Black girl.

That specific truth wasn't always loud; it didn't shout its presence from the rooftops or erupt in visible conflict. It whispered. It pressed into me in ways I couldn't describe, a constant, low-frequency weight that I absorbed through my skin. It lived in the way eyes lingered too long, the way conversations subtly shifted when I entered a room, the unspoken rules of engagement that were never written down but were instantly understood. It was a kind of societal dog whistle—a resonant hum of historical context that only we could hear, a shared, silent understanding of the boundaries imposed upon us. It was a pervasive, subtle violence that didn't leave bruises, not physical ones, but irrevocably marked your spirit and your soul.

At South Bay Lutheran, the quiet halls of the small private school served as a stark contrast to the trauma I carried. No one there truly found me. I wasn't failing academically; my grades were solid, capable. But I wasn't being seen either. Not truly. Not the complex girl behind the mask I had perfected. I existed in a perpetual state of blending, a brown girl in a predominantly white world, a chameleon diligently adapting to its surroundings. If I achieved average grades, it was expected; it fit the convenient, non-threatening mold. If I coasted, sliding by without demanding attention, no one asked why. No one questioned the quiet girl in the back. The silence of the external world reinforced the silence of the internal world.

Yet, there were the rare, precious souls who saw past the surface. The teachers who would pull me aside, their voices low, their eyes kind, and say, "You're insanely smart. You're capable of so much more." The coaches who saw me. Always. Always saw the athlete. The raw strength. The sheer talent. And I had to ask the question that haunts so many Black women who excel: Is that the only reliable place a Black girl gets to be seen—on the court? On the track? In motion, sweating, performing, pushing her body to its absolute limits? Is performance the only currency by which we are permitted to earn our visibility?

Even that visibility felt utterly conditional. My talent wasn't celebrated as a personal gift to be nurtured for my own sake. It was used. It was used to prove a point. To shame the boys who couldn't lift as much as I could. To entertain the crowds. To win games. To serve a purpose entirely beyond my own core self. No one asked what I needed. No one asked what I was carrying. The invisible burdens. The silent screams. The crushing weight of performance and expectation.

Carrying Quieter

My personal trauma stayed buried, not because I was ashamed of the pain itself, but because I had learned, over and over, that I wasn't meant to be seen. Not fully. Not safely. My pain wasn't exceptional in the eyes of the world; it was expected. It was just another predictable part of the narrative, another statistic to be filed away. And that's the part that still breaks me decades later—the casual, profound acceptance of suffering. The way the larger world normalized our pain.

We don't cry louder in the face of this systemic indifference. We learn to carry quieter. It's not a choice we actively make; it's survival. We are forced to outwork, pushing harder and longer than anyone else. We outpray, sending desperate pleas into the silence. We outlast, simply by refusing to shatter. And sometimes, we don't even fully recognize the enormous effort of our own survival until we finally dare to tell the story. Until we give it a voice. Until we shine a light on the hidden corners.

That's why rap music hit me with the force of revelation. It was the raw, unfiltered truth, finally spoken out loud. Tupac, his voice a guttural cry, speaking of struggle and defiance. The raw ache of his song Brenda's Got a Baby, its story a devastating mirror of my own unspoken pain. The rhythm of truth, pulsing through the speakers, validated my experience. It was the brilliance of pain set to a beat, a melody that somehow made the suffering beautiful and universally legible.

There was no metaphor needed in that music. No flowery, self-protective language. Just the naked reality. It was a voice that made mine feel less alone, a voice that profoundly understood the architecture of my existence.

I didn't know then what I know now. That being Black isn't the weight—it's not the burden itself. It's the echo. It's the constant, subtle reverberation of history, of impossible expectation, of systemic judgment. It is the thing that follows you into every room, every school, every silence. It is the immutable lens through which the world chooses to see you, and through which you are forced to learn to see yourself.

This is not just a chapter about race. It's a chapter about being a girl who, by all accounts, wasn't supposed to survive—who carried the crushing weight of familial and historical trauma, who endured so much, and who, against all odds, did not break.

The Clarity of the Mirror

It's a chapter about learning that the mirror was never actually broken. Not truly. It was simply too fogged up—fogged up by years of unshed tears, by the paralyzing fear of exposure, by the dust of unspoken truths. It was too obscured by the world's conditional expectations and my own diligently hidden pain. The mirror itself was fine; it was my lens that was fractured.

And now, after years of searching, after years of silence, after years of desperate hiding behind a perfected mask, I stand before that mirror. I see her.

She is Clear.

The Light is On.

She is Still Here. Still Burning. And ready, finally, to shine.

This profound realization—that survival is not invisibility, but unapologetic presence—is the true foundation of my life's work. The girl who ran away to Chico State has returned, not from the external chaos, but from the internal shadow. The final piece of the armor is not silence, but truth. I was only 18 years old so I didn't know exactly what the world held for me.

What I knew was what I was not,

Who I was not

The rest woould have to just wait and see........